MENTAL PRESSURE

MASTERING STRESS TO ACHIEVE SUCCESS AND HAPPINESS

RAHUL DWIVEDI

Contents

Preface

As individuals, we all face pressures in our lives – some external, others internal. These pressures can stem from our peers, academics, social norms, family expectations, romantic relationships, self-identity struggles, or even substance use temptations. Often, these pressures intertwine, creating a complex web of challenges that can feel overwhelming and inescapable.

My journey with navigating pressures began in my late teens. As a bright student, I faced immense academic pressure to excel. Simultaneously, I grappled with peer pressure to conform to certain social norms and engage in activities that didn't align with my values. The conflicting demands of excelling academically while fitting in with my peers took a toll on my mental health and self-confidence.

During this tumultuous period, I found solace in the unconditional support of my family. However, their well-intentioned expectations and aspirations for my future added another layer of pressure. I felt torn between fulfilling their dreams and carving my path, a dilemma many young adults face.

As I navigated these challenges, I realized that pressures are not isolated experiences; they are interconnected and can have far-reaching impacts on individuals, communities, and societies. This realization motivated me to delve deeper into the various pressures faced by people across India and globally.

Through extensive research and engagement with government data, I discovered alarming trends and statistics that shed light on the pervasive nature of these pressures. For instance, a recent National Crime Records Bureau report revealed that nearly one in four students in India experience high levels of academic pressure, leading to mental health issues and, in some cases, tragic consequences.

Moreover, the pressures faced by individuals are not limited to specific age groups or demographics. They permeate all aspects of life, from childhood to adulthood, cutting across socioeconomic strata and cultural boundaries.

It became evident that addressing these pressures requires a holistic approach – one that acknowledges their interconnectedness and seeks to provide comprehensive solutions. This book aims to do just that, by exploring the various pressures individuals face, delving into authentic government data, and presenting real-life stories that resonate with readers from diverse backgrounds.

Through this journey, we will uncover the challenges and existing problems, and more importantly, we will explore practical solutions and strategies for navigating these pressures. We will also examine the way forward, advocating for systemic changes, policy reforms, and individual empowerment to create a society where individuals can thrive without the debilitating weight of external and internal pressures.

Ultimately, this book is a call to action – a clarion call to acknowledge and address the pressures that impede our collective well-being. By understanding the gravity of these pressures and embracing a holistic approach to overcoming them, we can pave the way for a more fulfilling and pressure-free life, not just for ourselves, but for generations to come.

Acknowledgements

I extend my heartfelt gratitude to all those who have supported me on this journey. To my family, for their unwavering love and encouragement; to my friends, for their understanding and patience; to the mentors and teachers who guided me; and to every individual who shared their story with me, inspiring the creation of this book.

Lastly, to you, the reader – thank you for embarking on this journey with me. I hope that the insights and strategies shared within these pages will empower you to navigate life's pressures with resilience and grace.

With sincere thanks,

Rahul Dwivedi

My Journey: From Aspiring Civil Servants To Empowering Storyteller

As I reflect on the winding path that has brought me to this moment, I am filled with a profound sense of gratitude and purpose. What began as a burning desire to serve my nation as a civil servant through the prestigious UPSC examinations has evolved into a mission to empower and inspire through the power of storytelling.

My journey started with unwavering determination and an unquenchable thirst for knowledge. Fueled by a dream to contribute to the betterment of society, I devoted countless hours to studying, meticulously preparing for the rigorous UPSC exams that stood before me like an imposing mountain to conquer.

With a strong foundation from my 12th-grade studies, I pursued a Bachelor's and Master's degree in Arts from Bhopal, relying on self-study and an unwavering spirit. My sights were set firmly on the prize, and I was willing to do whatever it took to achieve my goal.

Yet, despite my best efforts and countless sacrifices, success in the UPSC examinations remained elusive. The weight of disappointment was palpable, but it also catalyzed self-reflection and growth. It was during this time of introspection that I realized the importance of proper guidance and mentorship – a crucial component that had been missing from my journey.

However, from every setback emerges an opportunity for transformation. It was during this period of soul-searching that I discovered my true passion – the art of storytelling. As a self-proclaimed generalist with a thirst for knowledge on a vast array of subjects, I found solace in the written word, using it as a vehicle to share my experiences, insights, and hard-won wisdom with others.

And so, the idea for this book was born – a labour of love, born from the ashes of disappointment and forged in the fires of determination. Through these pages, I aim to shed light on the immense pressures faced by individuals, from peer pressure and academic demands to social expectations and more. I seek to provide practical strategies and solutions for navigating these challenges with grace and resilience.

My mission is clear – to be the mentor that I wish I had during my tumultuous journey. I seek to empower individuals, parents, educators, and policymakers alike with the knowledge and tools they need to nurture well-being and success, regardless of the pressures they face.

As you journey with me through these pages, I invite you to embrace the complexities of life's pressures, learn from the stories shared within, and envision a brighter future for all. Together, let us embark on a quest to provide the guidance and support that individuals so desperately need and deserve.

With unwavering determination and a heart full of hope,

How This Book Will Benefit You

"**Mental Pressure:** Mastering Stress to Achieve Success and Happiness" is not just a book; it is a lifeline for those drowning in the turbulent waters of psychological stress. This book promises to provide a comprehensive understanding of mental pressure, its causes, and its effects. More importantly, it offers practical strategies and solutions to navigate and overcome these challenges.

What Readers Will Gain:

1. **Awareness and Understanding:** Through a blend of personal stories, scientific research, and expert insights, readers will gain a deep understanding of mental pressure and its various facets. You will learn how to identify the sources of your stress and recognize its impact on your life.
2. **Practical Tools and Techniques:** This book is packed with actionable advice and proven techniques to manage and reduce mental pressure. From mindfulness practices and time management strategies to resilience-building exercises, you will discover tools that can be immediately applied to improve your mental well-being.
3. **Empathy and Relatability:** By sharing real-life stories, including my own journey and those of others who have faced similar struggles, this book aims to create a sense of connection and empathy. You will realize that you are not alone in your experiences and that others have successfully navigated similar challenges.
4. **Guidance for Specific Groups:** Recognizing that mental pressure affects different demographics in unique ways, this book includes tailored advice for students, working professionals, and parents. Each section is designed to address the specific pressures faced by these groups and offer relevant coping strategies.
5. **Long-Term Solutions and Systemic Change:** Beyond individual strategies, this book advocates for systemic changes and policy reforms that can help alleviate mental pressure on a broader scale. Readers will be inspired to contribute to creating a more supportive and understanding society.

6. **Empowerment and Hope**: Ultimately, this book is about empowerment. It aims to equip you with the knowledge and confidence to face life's pressures head-on, fostering a sense of hope and resilience. By mastering mental pressure, you can achieve not only success but also true happiness and fulfilment.

Introduction

According to the National Crime Records Bureau of India, in 2019 alone, more than 10,000 students took their own lives, citing academic stress as a significant factor. This heartbreaking statistic underscores a global epidemic that transcends geographical boundaries, affecting millions of individuals irrespective of their age, gender, or socio-economic status. Mental pressure is an omnipresent force, shaping and often distorting the lives of those it grips.

Definition of Mental Pressure and Its Relevance Today

Mental pressure, often referred to as psychological stress, encompasses a wide range of emotional and cognitive strains that individuals face due to various internal and external factors. This pressure can manifest in numerous ways, including anxiety, depression, burnout, and physical health issues. In today's fast-paced and highly competitive world, the sources of mental pressure are manifold:

Academic Demands: Students at all levels are under constant pressure to achieve high grades, secure prestigious scholarships, and gain admission to top-tier institutions.

Workplace Stress: Professionals are expected to meet tight deadlines, excel in their roles, and continually outperform their peers to climb the corporate ladder.

Social Media and Peer Pressure: The pervasive influence of social media has created an environment where individuals feel compelled to present a perfect image, leading to comparisons and a sense of inadequacy.

Family Expectations: Parental aspirations and societal norms can impose additional burdens, especially in cultures where familial success is closely tied to individual achievements.

Economic Uncertainty: Financial instability and the pressure to secure a stable future add another layer of stress, affecting mental well-being.

In a world where success is often quantified by material achievements and social validation, mental pressure has become an almost inevitable byproduct of modern life. The relevance of addressing mental pressure today cannot be overstated. The COVID-19 pandemic has further exacerbated these pressures, as individuals grapple with isolation, job losses, and an uncertain future.

UNDERSTANDING MENTAL PRESSURE

Mental pressure, commonly known as psychological stress, refers to the emotional and cognitive strain individuals experience due to various internal and external factors. It is the body's response to demands or threats that are perceived as overwhelming or challenging. While some degree of stress can be motivating and even beneficial, chronic or excessive mental pressure can lead to a range of negative outcomes, including anxiety, depression, burnout, and physical health issues. Mental pressure can stem from numerous sources, such as academic demands, workplace responsibilities, social relationships, financial instability, and personal expectations.

Importance of Understanding Mental Pressure in Today's Context

In today's fast-paced and highly competitive world, understanding mental pressure is more important than ever. The digital age, with its constant connectivity and social media influence, has added new dimensions to the pressures individuals face. Students are under immense pressure to excel academically and secure future opportunities, while professionals grapple with high-performance expectations and work-life balance challenges. Additionally, societal and familial expectations can impose significant stress, particularly in cultures where success is closely tied to individual achievements.

The COVID-19 pandemic has further highlighted the importance of addressing mental pressure. Lockdowns, social isolation, economic uncertainty, and health concerns have exacerbated stress levels globally, making mental well-being a critical issue. By comprehensively understanding mental pressure, its sources, and its impacts, individuals and societies can develop effective strategies to manage stress and promote mental health. This knowledge is vital for creating supportive environments in schools, workplaces, and communities, where individuals can thrive without being overwhelmed by the demands of modern life.

In this chapter, we will delve into the definition, types, and historical context of mental pressure, supported by scientific research and expert opinions. We will also explore personal stories and examples that illustrate the real-world impact of mental pressure, setting the stage for practical solutions in the subsequent chapters.

What is Mental Pressure?

Mental pressure, commonly referred to as psychological stress, is the emotional and cognitive strain that arises when individuals perceive that they cannot adequately cope with the demands placed upon them. This pressure can stem from various sources, including work, school, relationships, financial challenges, and personal expectations. When faced with a stressor, the body activates a series of physiological responses, such as the release of adrenaline and cortisol, which prepare the individual to handle the perceived threat. While this response can be beneficial in short-term situations, prolonged exposure to stress can lead to significant mental and physical health issues, including anxiety, depression, cardiovascular diseases, and impaired cognitive function.

Types of Mental Pressure

Acute Stress

Acute stress is a short-term form of stress that arises from specific events or situations perceived as immediate threats. This type of stress triggers the body's fight-or-flight response, preparing individuals to respond quickly to danger. For example, a person might experience acute stress when narrowly avoiding a car accident or during a high-stakes job interview. The physiological symptoms of acute stress can include increased heart rate, heightened senses, and a surge of adrenaline. While acute stress is a natural and often necessary response to immediate challenges, it typically dissipates once the threat has passed. According to the American Psychological Association, acute stress can be beneficial in certain scenarios by enhancing alertness and performance in critical situations.

Chronic Stress

Chronic stress occurs when individuals are exposed to prolonged periods of stress without adequate relief or coping mechanisms. This type of stress is often related to ongoing situations such as financial difficulties, long-term illness, or an unsatisfying job. Unlike acute stress, chronic stress can wear down the body and mind over time, leading to serious health problems such as heart disease, hypertension, and mental health disorders like depression and anxiety. For example, a study published in the Journal of Occupational Health Psychology found that individuals experiencing chronic work-related stress exhibited higher levels of burnout and job dissatisfaction. Chronic stress can also weaken the immune system, making individuals more susceptible to illnesses. It requires comprehensive management strategies to mitigate its long-term effects.

Episodic Acute Stress

Episodic acute stress is characterized by frequent episodes of acute stress. Individuals who experience this type of stress often live chaotic and crisis-driven lives, constantly moving from one stressful situation to another. This pattern can result in persistent tension and anxiety, leading to an overall negative impact on health and well-being. For example, someone with a high-pressure job that involves constant deadlines and unpredictable demands might experience episodic acute stress. According to the Mayo Clinic, people with episodic acute stress may feel perpetually rushed, irritable, and anxious, often struggling to maintain a balance between work and personal life. This type of stress requires intervention to prevent it from escalating into chronic stress.

Traumatic Stress

Traumatic stress occurs in response to a deeply distressing or disturbing event, such as a natural disaster, serious accident, or personal assault. This type of stress can lead to long-lasting psychological impacts, including Post-Traumatic Stress Disorder (PTSD). Traumatic stress can disrupt an individual's ability to function normally and may cause symptoms such as flashbacks, nightmares, severe anxiety, and uncontrollable thoughts about the event. For instance, veterans returning from combat often experience traumatic stress and may struggle with PTSD as a result. According to the National Institute of Mental Health (NIMH), treatment for traumatic stress often involves therapy and, in some cases, medication to help manage symptoms and facilitate recovery.

Examples and Brief Anecdotes for Each Type

Acute Stress Example: Emma, a nurse working in an emergency room, often experiences acute stress during high-pressure situations where she must make quick decisions to save lives. Despite the intense nature of her job, she finds that the stress subsides after her shifts, allowing her to return to a state of normalcy.

Chronic Stress Example: John, a middle-aged man, has been working in a toxic work environment for several years, facing constant criticism and unrealistic expectations from his boss. This ongoing stress has led to chronic health issues, including hypertension and anxiety, severely impacting his quality of life.

Episodic Acute Stress Example: Sara, a financial analyst, frequently deals with episodic acute stress due to the unpredictable nature of the stock market and the constant pressure to perform. Her high-stress job often leaves her feeling rushed and overwhelmed, impacting her personal relationships and overall well-being.

Traumatic Stress Example: Michael, a soldier returning from combat, struggles with traumatic stress and PTSD. He experiences flashbacks and severe anxiety related to his time in the war zone, making it difficult for him to reintegrate into civilian life.

Historical Context of Mental Pressure

Ancient and Historical Perspectives on Stress

In ancient times, the concept of stress was closely tied to physical threats and survival. Early humans experienced stress in response to immediate dangers such as predators or environmental hazards. This type of stress triggered the "fight-or-flight" response, which was crucial for survival. The ancient Greeks and Romans, although not using the term "stress" as we do today, recognized the impact of emotions and external pressures on well-being. Hippocrates, known as the father of medicine, suggested that an imbalance in bodily fluids, or humors, could cause both physical and psychological distress.

In Eastern traditions, such as ancient Chinese and Indian medicine, stress was understood in the context of balance and harmony. The concept of "Qi" in Chinese medicine and the principle of "doshas" in Ayurveda emphasized maintaining balance within the body to prevent illness, including psychological distress. Meditation and mindfulness practices were developed as methods to achieve mental calmness and resilience against stress.

Evolution of Stress Understanding in the 20ᵗʰ Century

The modern scientific understanding of stress began to take shape in the early 20ᵗʰ century. In the 1930s, Hungarian endocrinologist Hans Selye conducted pioneering research that laid the foundation for contemporary stress theory. Selye introduced the term "stress" to describe the body's nonspecific response to demands or threats. He developed the General Adaptation Syndrome (GAS) model, which outlines three stages of stress response: alarm, resistance, and exhaustion. Selye's work highlighted the physiological effects of chronic stress, emphasizing its potential to cause long-term harm.

During World War II, the psychological impact of combat stress on soldiers brought further attention to the field. The term "combat fatigue" or "shell shock" was used to describe what we now recognize as Post-Traumatic Stress Disorder (PTSD). The war spurred significant research into the effects of acute and traumatic stress, leading to the development of better treatment and support systems for affected individuals.

In the latter half of the 20ᵗʰ century, psychologists such as Richard Lazarus advanced the understanding of stress by focusing on cognitive appraisal. Lazarus proposed that stress is a result of an individual's perception of a situation and their perceived ability to cope with it. This cognitive approach underscored the importance of subjective experience in stress and led to the development of stress management techniques that focus on changing perceptions and coping mechanisms.

Modern-Day Stressors and Their Historical Roots

Today, the sources of mental pressure have evolved but still have roots in historical contexts. The rapid advancement of technology and globalization has introduced new stressors, such as constant connectivity, information overload, and the pressure to maintain a social media presence. These modern-day stressors can be traced back to historical developments in communication and commerce.

For example, the Industrial Revolution brought about significant changes in work patterns and social structures. The shift from agrarian economies to industrial production created new forms of workplace stress, including long hours, repetitive tasks, and job insecurity. These stressors laid the groundwork for contemporary work-related stress issues, such as burnout and work-life imbalance.

Similarly, the evolution of social norms and expectations has contributed to the current landscape of mental pressure. In many cultures, historical emphasis on academic achievement, professional success, and social status has intensified, leading to heightened stress in educational and professional settings. The societal pressure to conform to certain standards and achieve specific milestones can be traced back to historical ideals of success and accomplishment.

Moreover, economic instability and financial pressures have deep historical roots. The Great Depression of the 1930s highlighted the profound impact of economic downturns on mental health, a theme that continues to resonate in today's global economy. The recurring cycles of economic booms and busts perpetuate financial anxiety and stress, affecting individuals' mental well-being across generations.

By understanding the historical context of mental pressure, we can better appreciate how past experiences and developments shape our current challenges. This awareness allows us to develop more effective strategies to address and manage stress in the modern world.

Physiology of Stress

Fight-or-Flight Response

The fight-or-flight response is a physiological reaction that occurs in response to perceived harmful events, attacks, or threats to survival. Coined by physiologist Walter Cannon in the early 20th century, this response involves a series of hormonal and physiological changes designed to prepare the body to either confront or flee from danger.

When an individual perceives a threat, the hypothalamus in the brain triggers the release of adrenaline and noradrenaline from the adrenal glands. These hormones rapidly prepare the body for action by increasing heart rate, elevating blood pressure, and boosting energy supplies. Blood flow is redirected to essential muscles, the respiratory rate increases and glucose levels rise to provide immediate energy.

Simultaneously, the hypothalamus activates the HPA (hypothalamic-pituitary-adrenal) axis, leading to the release of cortisol, a stress hormone. Cortisol helps maintain fluid balance and blood pressure while regulating key functions that are not essential in a fight-or-flight situation, such as immune responses and digestion. These combined hormonal responses enhance an individual's ability to respond swiftly and effectively to threats.

While the fight-or-flight response is crucial for survival in immediate danger, it is not as beneficial when activated repeatedly in response to non-life-threatening stressors. In modern life, this response can be triggered by various psychological pressures, such as work deadlines or social conflicts, leading to chronic activation that can harm health over time.

Impact of Chronic Stress on the Body

Chronic stress occurs when the body's fight-or-flight response is activated repeatedly over an extended period, without sufficient recovery time. This prolonged activation can have numerous detrimental effects on physical and mental health.

Physiologically, chronic stress can lead to elevated cortisol levels, which, over time, can suppress the immune system, increase blood pressure, and raise the risk of cardiovascular diseases. Chronic stress is also associated with the development of metabolic disorders, such as obesity and diabetes, due to its impact on insulin regulation and fat storage. Furthermore, sustained high cortisol levels can cause muscle tension and pain, headaches, and gastrointestinal issues like irritable bowel syndrome.

The brain is particularly vulnerable to the effects of chronic stress. Research has shown that prolonged stress can impair cognitive functions, such as memory and learning, by affecting the hippocampus, a brain region involved in these processes. Chronic stress can also alter the brain's structure and function, increasing the risk of mental health disorders like anxiety, depression, and PTSD.

A study published in the journal Psychoneuroendocrinology highlighted that chronic stress could reduce neurogenesis (the formation of new neurons) in the hippocampus, leading to cognitive decline and increased susceptibility to mental health conditions. Additionally, chronic stress can exacerbate pre-existing health conditions, making it a significant public health concern.

Expert Opinion: Dr. Robert Sapolsky's Research

Dr. Robert Sapolsky, a renowned neuroscientist and professor at Stanford University, has extensively studied the effects of chronic stress on the brain and body. His research has significantly advanced our understanding of how prolonged exposure to stress hormones impacts overall health.

In his seminal work, Why Zebras Don't Get Ulcers, Dr. Sapolsky explains that while acute stress responses are essential for survival, chronic stress can have harmful effects. He emphasizes that humans, unlike animals, often experience stress from psychological and social pressures, which can trigger chronic stress responses even in the absence of immediate physical threats.

Dr. Sapolsky's research has shown that chronic stress can lead to the atrophy of neurons in the hippocampus, reducing its volume and impairing cognitive functions such as memory and spatial navigation. His studies also indicate that chronic stress can disrupt the prefrontal cortex, the brain region responsible for executive functions, including decision-making, impulse control, and social behaviour.

In a study published in Nature Reviews Neuroscience, Dr. Sapolsky and his colleagues demonstrated that chronic stress could increase the vulnerability of neurons to damage and death, contributing to neurodegenerative diseases like Alzheimer's. Moreover, his research highlights the role of stress in exacerbating mental health disorders, as chronic exposure to cortisol can lead to changes in brain chemistry and structure that predispose individuals to anxiety and depression.

Dr. Sapolsky advocates for stress management techniques, such as mindfulness, exercise, and social support, to mitigate the adverse effects of chronic stress. His work underscores the importance of addressing psychological stressors in modern life to promote better mental and physical health.

Psychological Impact of Stress

Cognitive Appraisal Model by Richard Lazarus

Richard Lazarus, a pioneering psychologist, developed the cognitive appraisal model to explain the psychological mechanisms of stress. According to Lazarus, stress is not merely a result of external events but is significantly influenced by how individuals perceive and interpret these events. This model consists of two key components: primary appraisal and secondary appraisal.

In primary appraisal, individuals assess whether an event or situation poses a threat to their well-being. This assessment determines if the event is perceived as irrelevant, benign-positive, or stressful. If deemed stressful, the event is further evaluated as a threat (potential for harm), a challenge (growth potential), or a loss (actual damage already occurred).

Secondary appraisal involves evaluating one's resources and options for coping with the stressor. This step assesses the individual's perceived ability to manage or alter the situation and mitigate the stress. The outcome of this appraisal determines the emotional response and the coping strategies employed.

Lazarus's model emphasizes that stress is a dynamic process involving continuous interaction between the individual and their environment. This cognitive approach highlights the importance of perception and interpretation in determining stress levels. For instance, two people might experience the same event, such as a job loss, but their stress responses will differ based on their appraisals of the situation and their perceived coping abilities.

Lazarus's research underscores the need for stress management techniques that focus on altering perceptions and enhancing coping strategies. Cognitive-behavioural therapy (CBT), which aims to change maladaptive thought patterns, is a practical application of this model in clinical settings.

Mental Health Disorders Linked to Chronic Stress

Chronic stress has been linked to a variety of mental health disorders, highlighting the profound impact prolonged stress can have on psychological well-being. Some of the most common mental health issues associated with chronic stress include anxiety disorders, depression, and Post-Traumatic Stress Disorder (PTSD).

Anxiety Disorders: Chronic stress can lead to persistent feelings of worry and fear, characteristic of anxiety disorders. Generalized Anxiety Disorder (GAD), panic disorder, and social anxiety disorder are often exacerbated by prolonged stress. According to the National Institute of Mental Health (NIMH), individuals with high levels of chronic stress are more likely to develop anxiety disorders, as constant stress disrupts normal brain function and increases the production of stress hormones.

Depression: There is a well-established link between chronic stress and depression. Prolonged exposure to stress can alter brain chemistry, particularly the balance of neurotransmitters like serotonin and dopamine, which regulate mood. Research published in the journal Biological Psychiatry indicates that chronic stress can lead to structural changes in the brain, such as a reduction in the size of the hippocampus, a region involved in mood regulation. These changes can contribute to the onset and persistence of depressive symptoms.

Post-Traumatic Stress Disorder (PTSD): Chronic stress resulting from traumatic events can lead to PTSD, characterized by intrusive memories, hyperarousal, and emotional numbing. The American Psychiatric Association notes that individuals exposed to prolonged or severe stressors, such as combat, natural disasters, or personal assaults, are at a higher risk of developing PTSD. The disorder can have long-term effects on mental health, affecting daily functioning and overall quality of life.

These mental health disorders illustrate the significant psychological impact of chronic stress. Early intervention and effective stress management strategies are crucial in mitigating these effects and promoting mental well-being.

Expert Opinion: American Psychological Association

The American Psychological Association (APA) has extensively researched and documented the effects of stress on mental health. According to the APA, chronic stress is a significant contributor to various psychological issues and can lead to long-term mental health problems if not adequately managed.

In its annual report, "Stress in America," the APA highlights the pervasive nature of stress in modern society and its impact on mental health. The report indicates that a majority of Americans experience high levels of stress, with significant sources including work, financial pressures, and personal relationships. The APA emphasizes that chronic stress can impair cognitive function, reduce emotional regulation, and increase vulnerability to mental health disorders.

Dr. Arthur C. Evans Jr., CEO of the APA, has stated that chronic stress affects both the mind and body, leading to a range of health issues. "Prolonged exposure to stress hormones like cortisol can disrupt almost all of your body's processes, increasing the risk of numerous health problems, including mental health disorders such as anxiety and depression," he explains. Dr. Evans advocates for comprehensive stress management strategies that include psychological support, lifestyle changes, and mindfulness practices to mitigate the adverse effects of stress.

The APA also underscores the importance of early intervention and the role of mental health professionals in addressing chronic stress. Techniques such as Cognitive-Behavioral Therapy (CBT) and Mindfulness-Based Stress Reduction (MBSR) are highlighted as effective approaches to help individuals manage stress and improve their mental health outcomes.

In summary, the APA's extensive research and expert opinions underscore the critical need for effective stress management interventions to protect mental health and enhance overall well-being.

Role of Resilience

Definition and Importance of Resilience

Resilience is the ability to adapt to and recover from adversity, stress, and challenging life events. It involves a dynamic process of facing difficulties, learning from them, and emerging stronger. Resilience is not an innate trait but rather a set of behaviours, thoughts, and actions that can be developed and strengthened over time.

The importance of resilience lies in its capacity to buffer the negative effects of stress and promote mental well-being. Resilient individuals are better equipped to manage stress, maintain a positive outlook, and sustain their physical and mental health despite facing significant challenges. Resilience helps people navigate through life's inevitable ups and downs, allowing them to cope with crises, recover from setbacks, and adapt to new circumstances.

Research has shown that resilience is associated with numerous positive outcomes, including lower levels of anxiety and depression, improved coping skills, and greater life satisfaction. For example, a study published in the Journal of Personality and Social Psychology found that resilient individuals experience fewer symptoms of depression and anxiety following stressful life events compared to those with lower resilience levels.

Building resilience involves fostering a supportive social network, maintaining a sense of purpose, and developing problem-solving skills. Practices such as mindfulness, physical exercise, and seeking professional help when needed also contribute to enhancing resilience. By cultivating these traits and behaviours, individuals can better manage stress and lead healthier, more fulfilling lives.

Expert Opinion: Dr. Ann Masten's Research

Dr. Ann Masten, a leading expert on resilience and a professor at the University of Minnesota, has conducted extensive research on resilience in children and families. Her work has significantly advanced the understanding of resilience as a developmental process that can be nurtured and strengthened.

In her influential book, Ordinary Magic: Resilience in Development, Dr. Masten describes resilience as "ordinary magic," emphasizing that it is a common and natural response to adversity. She argues that resilience arises from the interplay of individual characteristics, supportive relationships, and external resources. According to Dr. Masten, key factors that contribute to resilience include positive attachment relationships, effective caregiving, and access to educational and community resources.

Dr. Masten's research highlights the importance of protective factors that help individuals overcome adversity. These factors include having a supportive family environment, access to quality education, and opportunities for skill development. Her studies have shown that children who grow up in nurturing environments with strong support systems are more likely to develop resilience and succeed despite facing significant challenges.

In a study published in the Annual Review of Psychology, Dr. Masten and her colleagues examined the resilience processes in children exposed to chronic stress and trauma. The study found that children who had supportive relationships and stable caregiving showed better adaptive functioning and fewer psychological problems compared to those without such support. This research underscores the critical role of positive relationships and stable environments in fostering resilience.

Dr. Masten advocates for policies and interventions that strengthen resilience at the individual, family, and community levels. She emphasizes the need for accessible mental health services, educational programs, and community support systems to help individuals build resilience and thrive despite adversity.

Mindfulness and Stress Reduction

Benefits of Mindfulness Practices

Mindfulness is the practice of intentionally focusing attention on the present moment and accepting it without judgment. This mental state can be cultivated through various techniques, such as meditation, breathing exercises, and mindful movement. The benefits of mindfulness practices for stress reduction and overall mental well-being are well-documented and widely recognized in both scientific research and clinical practice.

One of the primary benefits of mindfulness is its ability to reduce stress. By fostering a non-judgmental awareness of the present moment, mindfulness helps individuals detach from their automatic stress responses and gain perspective on their thoughts and feelings. This can lead to a significant reduction in the physiological symptoms of stress, such as elevated heart rate and blood pressure.

Research has shown that mindfulness practices can improve emotional regulation by enhancing the brain's ability to manage emotions and reduce reactivity to stressful situations. A study published in Health Psychology found that individuals who engaged in mindfulness meditation experienced lower levels of cortisol, the stress hormone, compared to those who did not practice mindfulness.

Additionally, mindfulness has been linked to improved mental health outcomes, including reduced symptoms of anxiety and depression. By encouraging a focus on the present moment and promoting a non-judgmental attitude, mindfulness helps individuals break free from cycles of rumination and negative thought patterns. A meta-analysis published in JAMA Internal Medicine reported that mindfulness-based interventions were effective in reducing symptoms of anxiety, depression, and stress.

Mindfulness also enhances cognitive functions such as attention, memory, and executive functioning. By training the mind to focus and remain present, mindfulness can improve concentration and decision-making skills, which are often impaired by stress.

Overall, mindfulness practices offer a holistic approach to stress reduction, promoting both mental and physical health benefits that contribute to overall well-being.

Expert Opinion: Dr. Jon Kabat-Zinn's Research on MBSR

Dr. Jon Kabat-Zinn, a pioneer in the field of mindfulness, developed the Mindfulness-Based Stress Reduction (MBSR) program in the late 1970s at the University of Massachusetts Medical School. MBSR is an evidence-based program designed to help individuals manage stress, pain, and illness through mindfulness practices. Dr. Kabat-Zinn's work has been instrumental in bringing mindfulness into mainstream medicine and psychology.

The MBSR program typically consists of an 8-week course that includes weekly group sessions, daily home practice, and a one-day retreat. Participants are taught various mindfulness techniques, such as body scan meditation, sitting meditation, and mindful yoga, which help them cultivate greater awareness and acceptance of the present moment.

Dr. Kabat-Zinn's research has demonstrated the profound impact of MBSR on stress reduction and overall health. In a landmark study published in General Hospital Psychiatry, participants in the MBSR program reported significant reductions in symptoms of anxiety and depression, as well as improvements in overall well-being. These benefits were maintained for up to three years following the intervention, indicating the long-term effectiveness of MBSR.

Further research has shown that MBSR can lead to structural and functional changes in the brain. A study conducted by researchers at Harvard Medical School found that participants who completed the MBSR program exhibited increased gray matter density in brain regions associated with learning, memory, and emotional regulation. These findings suggest that mindfulness practice can enhance brain plasticity and improve cognitive and emotional functioning.

Dr. Kabat-Zinn's work has also highlighted the role of mindfulness in managing chronic pain. In a study published in the Journal of Behavioral Medicine, patients with chronic pain who participated in the MBSR program reported significant reductions in pain intensity and improvements in their ability to cope with pain.

Overall, Dr. Kabat-Zinn's research underscores the efficacy of mindfulness-based interventions like MBSR in reducing stress, enhancing mental health, and promoting overall well-being. His contributions have paved the way for the widespread adoption of mindfulness practices in clinical and therapeutic settings.

Personal Stories and Examples

Arjun's Academic Pressure: Student Stress and Academic Expectations in India

Arjun Singh, a 17-year-old high school student from Bangalore, India, faced immense academic pressure to excel in his studies. As a top performer in his class, Arjun was under constant pressure from his parents, teachers, and peers to secure high marks and gain admission to a prestigious university. The competition was fierce, with thousands of students vying for limited spots in top institutions.

Arjun's day began at 5 a.m. with early morning coaching classes, followed by a full day of school and evening tuition sessions. Despite his best efforts, the fear of not meeting expectations loomed large, causing him significant stress and anxiety. He often experienced sleepless nights, worrying about upcoming exams and the future.

A report by the National Crime Records Bureau (NCRB) highlighted that academic pressure is a leading cause of stress among Indian students, with nearly 10,000 student suicides reported annually. Arjun's story is a stark reminder of the detrimental effects of extreme academic expectations. To cope, Arjun sought support from a school counsellor who helped him develop stress management techniques and realistic goals. With time, he learned to balance his studies and personal well-being, ultimately securing admission to a reputable college without compromising his mental health.

Maya's Workplace Stress: Professional Stress and Health Impacts

Maya Patel, a 35-year-old marketing executive in Mumbai, experienced chronic workplace stress due to high job demands and long working hours. As a project manager in a fast-paced advertising agency, Maya was responsible for overseeing multiple campaigns simultaneously, often working late nights and weekends to meet tight deadlines.

The pressure to perform and the fear of job loss led to significant stress, manifesting in physical symptoms such as frequent migraines, insomnia, and high blood pressure. Maya's work environment was highly competitive, with constant scrutiny and expectations to deliver exceptional results, contributing to her stress.

A study published in the Indian Journal of Occupational and Environmental Medicine found that workplace stress is a significant issue in India's corporate sector, affecting employees' mental and physical health. Maya's story reflects these findings, emphasizing the need for better workplace policies and support systems.

Recognizing the impact on her health, Maya sought help from a mental health professional who introduced her to mindfulness practices and stress management techniques. With these tools, Maya learned to set boundaries, delegate tasks, and prioritize self-care. Her company also introduced wellness programs, including flexible working hours and employee support groups, which helped Maya manage her stress more effectively.

Raj's Financial Worries: Economic Instability and Mental Health

Raj Kumar, a 45-year-old factory worker from Chennai, faced chronic financial instability due to low wages and irregular work hours. As the sole breadwinner for his family, Raj struggled to make ends meet, often worrying about providing for his wife and three children. The constant stress of financial insecurity took a toll on his mental health, leading to anxiety and depression.

According to a report by the World Health Organization (WHO), financial stress is a significant contributor to mental health issues globally. Raj's story is a poignant example of this reality. Despite working long hours, Raj's income was insufficient to cover basic expenses, let alone save for emergencies or the future.

To address his financial worries, Raj attended community workshops on financial literacy and management. These workshops, organized by local non-profits, provided valuable insights into budgeting, saving, and accessing social welfare schemes. Raj also received support from a mental health counsellor who helped him develop coping strategies for his anxiety and depression.

Through these interventions, Raj gradually improved his financial situation and mental health. He started a small side business to supplement his income and learned to manage his stress more effectively. Raj's story highlights the importance of financial education and mental health support in addressing economic instability.

Anita's Social Media Struggles: Impact of Social Media on Self-Esteem

Anita Verma, a 22-year-old university student from Delhi, struggled with the impact of social media on her self-esteem. Constantly exposed to curated images of perfection on platforms like Instagram and Facebook, Anita felt inadequate and insecure about her own life. The pressure to maintain an ideal online persona led to feelings of loneliness, anxiety, and low self-esteem.

A study by the Pew Research Center found that excessive social media use is linked to negative mental health outcomes, particularly among young adults. Anita's experience reflects these findings, as she spent hours scrolling through social media, comparing herself to peers and influencers who seemed to lead flawless lives.

Recognizing the detrimental impact on her mental health, Anita decided to take a digital detox. She reduced her social media usage and unfollowed accounts that made her feel insecure and focused on building real-life connections. She also engaged in activities that boosted her self-esteem, such as volunteering and joining a university club.

Anita sought support from a therapist who helped her develop a healthier relationship with social media. Through therapy, she learned to challenge negative thought patterns and appreciate her unique qualities and achievements. Anita's journey underscores the importance of mindful social media use and the need for mental health support to combat its negative effects.

Reena's Family Expectations: Cultural and Familial Pressures

Reena Sharma, a 28-year-old software engineer from Jaipur, faced significant cultural and familial pressures. Her family had high expectations for her to excel in her career and get married by a certain age. Balancing these expectations with her aspirations caused Reena considerable stress and anxiety.

In many cultures, family expectations play a crucial role in shaping individuals' lives, often leading to stress and conflict. Reena's story is a common one, as she felt torn between fulfilling her family's wishes and pursuing her own goals. The pressure to marry and achieve professional success simultaneously was overwhelming.

A report by the Lancet Psychiatry highlighted that cultural pressures significantly impact mental health, with individuals from collectivist cultures experiencing higher levels of stress due to family expectations. Reena's experience aligns with these findings, as she struggled to navigate her family's demands while maintaining her independence.

To cope with these pressures, Reena sought guidance from a life coach who helped her set boundaries and communicate her needs effectively to her family. She also joined a support group for young professionals facing similar challenges, where she found solidarity and advice.

Through these efforts, Reena learned to balance her family's expectations with her desires, finding a middle ground that allowed her to pursue her career and personal life on her own terms. Her story highlights the importance of open communication and support in managing cultural and familial pressures.

Chapter Summary

- Types of Mental Pressure: Acute stress, chronic stress, episodic acute stress, and traumatic stress.
- Historical Context of Mental Pressure: Ancient and historical perspectives, 20th-century evolution, and modern-day stressors.
- Physiology of Stress: Fight-or-flight response, impact of chronic stress on the body, and Dr. Robert Sapolsky's research.
- Psychological Impact of Stress: Cognitive appraisal model by Richard Lazarus, mental health disorders linked to chronic stress, and expert opinion from the American Psychological Association.

CHAPTER TWO

The Causes of Mental Pressure

In this chapter, we will explore the myriad causes of mental pressure, delving into both external and internal factors that contribute to psychological stress. Understanding these causes is crucial because it allows us to identify the root sources of stress and develop effective strategies to manage and mitigate its impact on our lives. We will examine common external stressors such as workplace demands, academic pressure, social media influence, and financial instability. Additionally, we will explore internal factors, including personal expectations, perfectionism, relationship dynamics, health concerns, and cognitive and emotional patterns. By providing real-life case studies and examples, this chapter aims to illustrate how these factors manifest in everyday life and affect mental health.

Importance of Understanding the Causes of Mental Pressure

Understanding the causes of mental pressure is essential for several reasons. First, it empowers individuals to recognize and address the specific sources of their stress, leading to more targeted and effective interventions. Awareness of the underlying causes helps in developing personalized coping strategies that can alleviate stress and enhance overall well-being.

Second, comprehending the diverse origins of mental pressure fosters empathy and support within communities. By acknowledging that stress can stem from various external and internal factors, individuals can better understand and support each other in managing life's challenges. This collective understanding promotes a more compassionate and supportive environment, whether in the workplace, educational institutions, or within families and social circles.

Finally, identifying the causes of mental pressure is crucial for developing broader societal and policy interventions. By recognizing the systemic issues that contribute to stress, such as economic instability or unrealistic academic expectations, stakeholders can advocate for changes that reduce these pressures at a structural level. This holistic approach not only addresses individual stress but also creates healthier and more resilient communities.

In the following sections, we will delve deeper into the specific external and internal factors that contribute to mental pressure, supported by scientific research and real-life examples to provide a comprehensive understanding of this complex issue.

External Factors

Workplace Stress

High Job Demands and Tight Deadlines

Workplace stress is often driven by high job demands and tight deadlines, which can create a pressure-cooker environment. Employees are frequently expected to juggle multiple tasks simultaneously, complete projects within unrealistic timeframes, and consistently deliver high-quality work. This constant pressure to perform can lead to feelings of overwhelm, anxiety, and burnout.

Research published by the American Psychological Association (APA) highlights that job demands significantly contribute to stress, with employees reporting that excessive workloads and tight deadlines are primary stressors. When the demands of the job exceed an individual's capacity to cope, it can result in physical and mental health issues, including chronic fatigue, depression, and cardiovascular diseases.

Job Insecurity and Lack of Control

Another major contributor to workplace stress is job insecurity and a lack of control over one's work environment. Employees who feel uncertain about their job stability or who perceive a lack of autonomy in their roles often experience higher levels of stress. This insecurity can stem from various factors, such as organizational restructuring, economic downturns, or management changes.

The National Institute for Occupational Safety and Health (NIOSH) has identified job insecurity as a significant stressor that can lead to a range of adverse outcomes, including decreased job satisfaction, reduced productivity, and increased absenteeism. Additionally, a lack of control over work processes and decisions can exacerbate stress, as employees may feel powerless and undervalued in their roles. Empowering employees by involving them in decision-making and providing clear communication about job stability can help mitigate these stressors.

Case Study: Real-Life Example of Workplace Stress

Sarah, a marketing manager at a fast-paced advertising agency, constantly faced high job demands and tight deadlines. Despite her dedication, the relentless pressure to deliver results and the fear of losing her job during a company downsizing led to severe anxiety and stress-related health issues. Recognizing the toll it was taking on her well-being, Sarah sought help from a mental health professional and started Practicing mindfulness and time management techniques. Her company also introduced wellness programs and flexible work hours, which significantly improved her stress levels and overall job satisfaction.

Academic Pressure

Competition and High Expectations

Academic pressure is a prevalent stressor among students, driven by intense competition and high expectations from parents, teachers, and society. The pursuit of academic excellence often leads to a relentless focus on grades, standardized test scores, and college admissions. This competitive environment can create significant stress, as students strive to meet or exceed expectations.

A study by the National Center for Biotechnology Information (NCBI) found that students experiencing high academic pressure are more likely to suffer from anxiety, depression, and other mental health issues. The constant comparison with peers and the fear of not measuring up can erode self-esteem and lead to a sense of inadequacy.

Exam Stress and Academic Workload

Exam stress and the academic workload further compound the pressure on students. The preparation for and performance in exams are critical determinants of academic success, creating a high-stakes environment. Students often face extensive syllabi, multiple subjects, and continuous assessments, leading to long hours of study and inadequate rest.

Research published in The Lancet indicates that exam stress is a significant contributor to student mental health problems, with many students reporting physical symptoms such as headaches, sleep disturbances, and gastrointestinal issues. The overwhelming academic workload can also lead to burnout, characterized by exhaustion, cynicism, and reduced academic performance.

Case Study: Example of Academic Pressure

Anjali, a high school student in Delhi, faced immense academic pressure to secure top grades and gain admission to a prestigious university. The competition was fierce, and the fear of disappointing her parents and teachers weighed heavily on her. The stress of continuous exams and an overwhelming workload led to anxiety and panic attacks. Seeking help from a school counsellor, Anjali learned stress management techniques and time management skills, which helped her cope with the pressure. Her school also implemented wellness programs and workshops on mental health, providing much-needed support for students like Anjali.

Social Media and Digital Stress

Comparison and Fear of Missing Out (FOMO)

Social media platforms have become an integral part of daily life, but their pervasive influence often leads to significant stress. One of the primary stressors is the constant comparison with others, which can foster feelings of inadequacy and low self-esteem. Users frequently encounter idealized representations of others' lives, achievements, and appearances, leading to unrealistic expectations and dissatisfaction with their own lives.

The phenomenon known as Fear of Missing Out (FOMO) exacerbates this issue. FOMO is the anxiety that others are having more fun, leading more fulfilling lives, or acquiring more valuable experiences than oneself. This fear is heightened by the curated content on social media, where users selectively share highlights rather than everyday realities. According to a study published in Computers in Human Behavior, high levels of FOMO are associated with increased stress, anxiety, and depression. The study found that individuals who spend more time on social media are more likely to experience FOMO, leading to a vicious cycle of comparison and stress.

Cyberbullying and Online Harassment

Another significant source of digital stress is cyberbullying and online harassment. Unlike traditional bullying, cyberbullying can occur at any time and reach victims through multiple online channels, making it pervasive and relentless. This form of harassment includes spreading false rumours, sending threatening messages, and publicly humiliating victims on social platforms.

The impact of cyberbullying on mental health is profound. Victims often experience severe anxiety, depression, and in extreme cases, suicidal thoughts. The American Academy of Pediatrics (AAP) reports that adolescents who are cyberbullied are more likely to suffer from mental health issues and engage in self-harm. The anonymity provided by the internet often emboldens perpetrators, making it challenging to identify and stop cyberbullying.

Case Study: Example of Social Media Stress

Emily, a college student from New York, found herself constantly comparing her life to the seemingly perfect lives of her friends on Instagram. The constant exposure to their curated posts led to feelings of inadequacy and FOMO, causing Emily significant stress and anxiety.

Additionally, she became a target of cyberbullying, with anonymous users leaving hurtful comments on her posts. Seeking help from a counsellor, Emily learned to manage her social media use, focusing on positive interactions and setting boundaries. She also joined a support group for victims of cyberbullying, which helped her regain confidence and improve her mental health.

Economic and Financial Stress

Unemployment and Financial Instability

Economic stress is a significant contributor to mental pressure, particularly when it stems from unemployment and financial instability. The uncertainty of job loss or the inability to find stable employment can lead to chronic stress, anxiety, and depression. This stress is compounded by the pressure to meet basic needs and support family members.

The World Health Organization (WHO) highlights that financial instability and unemployment are major risk factors for mental health issues. Individuals facing economic hardships are more likely to experience feelings of helplessness, low self-esteem, and social isolation. The financial strain not only affects mental health but can also lead to physical health problems due to the inability to afford necessary healthcare.

Debt and Financial Obligations

Debt and ongoing financial obligations are additional sources of economic stress. High levels of debt, whether from student loans, credit cards, or mortgages, can create a persistent burden that impacts daily life. The stress of managing debt repayment, coupled with interest accumulation, can feel overwhelming and insurmountable.

A report by the American Psychological Association (APA) found that financial stress is one of the top sources of stress for Americans. The constant worry about meeting financial obligations, avoiding debt collectors, and maintaining credit scores can lead to chronic stress and associated health issues. This stress can impair decision-making, leading to a cycle of poor financial choices and increasing debt.

Case Study: Example of Economic Stress

Mark, a 40-year-old factory worker from Detroit, faced severe economic stress after being laid off during an economic downturn. The sudden loss of income and the inability to find new employment led to mounting debt and financial instability. The stress from his financial situation caused Mark significant anxiety and depression. He sought help from a local non-profit organization that provided financial counselling and job placement services. Through this support, Mark managed to secure a new job and develop a manageable plan for his debt, gradually improving his financial and mental health.

Internal Factors

Personal Expectations and Perfectionism

Setting High Personal Standards

Setting high personal standards is often seen as a positive trait, driving individuals to achieve their best. However, when these standards become excessively high or unrealistic, they can lead to significant stress and pressure. Perfectionism, the tendency to strive for flawlessness, can create an environment where anything less than perfect is deemed unacceptable. This mindset can lead to chronic dissatisfaction, even when achievements are objectively impressive.

A study published in the Journal of Counseling Psychology found that perfectionism is associated with a range of mental health issues, including anxiety, depression, and burnout. Individuals who set excessively high standards may also experience procrastination, as the fear of not meeting their own expectations can paralyze their ability to start or complete tasks. This constant pressure to meet unattainable goals can be mentally and physically exhausting, ultimately diminishing overall well-being.

Fear of Failure and Self-Criticism

Perfectionism is closely linked to a profound fear of failure and relentless self-criticism. Individuals with perfectionistic tendencies often equate their self-worth with their achievements, leading to an intense fear of making mistakes or falling short. This fear can manifest as chronic anxiety and avoidance behaviours, where individuals may shy away from challenges to avoid the risk of failure.

Self-criticism exacerbates this issue, as perfectionists tend to be their harshest critics. A study by the National Institute of Mental Health (NIMH) highlighted that self-criticism is a significant predictor of mental health problems, including depression and anxiety. This negative self-talk can create a vicious cycle, where each perceived failure reinforces feelings of inadequacy and further fuels perfectionistic tendencies.

Case Study: Example of Perfectionism Stress

Jessica, a 30-year-old lawyer from Boston, struggled with perfectionism throughout her academic and professional life. Despite her numerous accomplishments, she constantly set unrealistically high standards for herself. The fear of making mistakes led to severe anxiety and burnout, affecting her work performance and personal life. Realizing the toll it was taking on her mental health, Jessica sought therapy, where she learned to set more realistic goals and practice self-compassion. By gradually changing her mindset, Jessica was able to reduce her stress levels and improve her overall well-being.

Relationship Stress

Family Dynamics and Marital Issues

Family dynamics and marital issues are significant sources of relationship stress. Conflicts within the family, whether between spouses, parents children, or extended family members, can create a tense and stressful home environment. Marital issues such as communication breakdowns, financial disagreements, and differing expectations can strain relationships and lead to chronic stress.

A study published in the Journal of Family Psychology found that unresolved family conflicts and marital dissatisfaction are linked to increased levels of stress, anxiety, and depression. The emotional toll of constant arguments and unresolved issues can affect not only the individuals involved but also the overall family unit. Effective communication, conflict resolution skills, and professional counselling are essential in managing and mitigating family and marital stress.

Social Relationships and Peer Pressure

Social relationships and peer pressure can also contribute significantly to stress. Maintaining social connections is crucial for mental well-being, but it can also be a source of pressure. Peer pressure, the influence exerted by peers to conform to certain behaviours, values, or norms, can lead to stress, particularly among adolescents and young adults.

The American Psychological Association (APA) highlights that peer pressure can result in risky behaviours, such as substance use, or create stress from the need to fit in and be accepted. The constant comparison with peers and the desire to meet social expectations can lead to anxiety and self-esteem issues. Building a supportive social network and learning to set healthy boundaries are key strategies for managing social relationship stress.

Case Study: Example of Relationship Stress

David, a 45-year-old engineer from Chicago, experienced significant stress due to ongoing marital conflicts and strained relationships with his teenage children. The constant arguments at home affected his work performance and overall mental health. Seeking help from a family therapist, David and his family learned effective communication techniques and conflict-resolution strategies. Through therapy, they were able to address underlying issues and improve their relationships, significantly reducing the stress and creating a more harmonious home environment.

Health and Lifestyle Factors

Chronic Illness and Health Anxiety

Chronic illness and health anxiety are significant contributors to mental pressure. Chronic illnesses such as diabetes, heart disease, and autoimmune disorders require ongoing management and can significantly impact an individual's quality of life. The constant need to monitor symptoms, adhere to treatment plans, and attend medical appointments can be overwhelming and exhausting.

Health anxiety, also known as illness anxiety disorder, exacerbates this stress. Individuals with health anxiety are preoccupied with the fear of having or developing a serious illness, often misinterpreting normal bodily sensations as signs of severe health issues. This constant worry can lead to frequent doctor visits, excessive medical testing, and substantial emotional distress.

A study published in the Journal of Psychosomatic Research found that individuals with chronic illnesses who also experience high levels of health anxiety report poorer quality of life and higher levels of stress and depression. Effective management of chronic illness often requires a multidisciplinary approach, including medical treatment, mental health support, and lifestyle modifications.

Poor Lifestyle Choices (Diet, Exercise, Sleep)

Poor lifestyle choices can significantly contribute to stress and overall mental health. An unhealthy diet, lack of exercise, and insufficient sleep can all exacerbate stress levels and lead to a range of physical and psychological issues.

A diet high in processed foods, sugar, and unhealthy fats can lead to weight gain, energy crashes, and poor mental health. Conversely, a balanced diet rich in fruits, vegetables, lean proteins, and whole grains supports overall well-being and can help manage stress.

Physical activity is a well-documented stress reducer. Regular exercise releases endorphins, which are natural mood lifters. According to the Centers for Disease Control and Prevention (CDC), even moderate physical activity can reduce symptoms of anxiety and depression, improve sleep, and enhance overall mood.

Sleep is another critical factor. Chronic sleep deprivation can lead to heightened stress levels, cognitive impairment, and increased risk of mental health disorders. The National Sleep Foundation recommends that adults aim for 7-9 hours of sleep per night to maintain optimal health and reduce stress.

Case Study: Example of Health-Related Stress

Maria, a 50-year-old woman from Los Angeles, struggled with managing her diabetes while also dealing with health anxiety. Her constant worry about her blood sugar levels and potential complications led to frequent panic attacks and sleepless nights. With the help of her healthcare provider, Maria adopted a balanced diet and regular exercise routine, which improved her diabetes management. She also worked with a therapist to address her health anxiety, learning coping strategies to reduce her stress. These combined efforts significantly improved Maria's physical health and mental well-being.

Cognitive and Emotional Factors

Negative Thinking Patterns and Anxiety

Negative thinking patterns, also known as cognitive distortions, can significantly contribute to stress and anxiety. These patterns include all-or-nothing thinking, overgeneralization, Catastrophizing, and personalization. Such thoughts often lead individuals to interpret situations more negatively than they are, exacerbating feelings of anxiety and stress.

For instance, catastrophizing involves imagining the worst-case scenario, even if it's unlikely. This can lead to chronic anxiety and an inability to enjoy the present moment. A study published in Cognitive Therapy and Research found that individuals with high levels of cognitive distortions are more prone to anxiety and depression, highlighting the importance of addressing these thought patterns in stress management.

Emotional Regulation and Coping Skills

Effective emotional regulation and coping skills are essential for managing stress and maintaining mental health. Emotional regulation involves recognizing and managing one's emotions in a healthy way, preventing them from becoming overwhelming. Poor emotional regulation can lead to impulsive reactions, heightened stress, and mental health issues.

Coping skills, such as problem-solving, seeking social support, and using relaxation techniques, are strategies individuals use to handle stress. Developing these skills can improve resilience and reduce the impact of stress. According to the American Psychological Association (APA), individuals who practice good emotional regulation and coping skills experience lower levels of stress and better overall mental health.

Mindfulness and cognitive-behavioural techniques are effective methods for improving emotional regulation. These approaches help individuals become more aware of their thoughts and feelings, enabling them to respond to stressors more effectively.

Case Study: Example of Cognitive Stress

John, a 35-year-old teacher from Seattle, frequently experienced anxiety due to negative thinking patterns. He often catastrophized small issues, leading to chronic stress and difficulty in managing his daily responsibilities. With the help of a cognitive-behavioural therapist, John learned to identify and challenge his negative thoughts, replacing them with more balanced and realistic perspectives. He also Practiced mindfulness meditation, which helped him stay grounded in the present moment. Over time, John's anxiety levels decreased, and he developed healthier coping mechanisms to handle stress.

Case Studies and Real-Life Examples

Case Study 1: Workplace Stress

Name: Sarah Thompson

Background: Sarah is a 29-year-old project manager at a tech startup in San Francisco. She frequently works 60-hour weeks to meet tight deadlines and manage multiple projects simultaneously.

Stress Factors: High job demands, tight deadlines, job insecurity

Impact: Sarah's relentless workload and the pressure to perform led to chronic anxiety and insomnia. She often felt overwhelmed and feared losing her job during the company restructuring phases. Her physical health declined, manifesting in frequent migraines and digestive issues.

Intervention: Sarah's company introduced flexible working hours and employee wellness programs. She sought help from a mental health professional, who taught her mindfulness and time management techniques. These changes helped Sarah reduce her stress levels and improve her overall well-being.

Case Study 2: Academic Pressure

Name: Arjun Singh

Background: Arjun is a 17-year-old high school student in Bangalore, India. He is a top performer under immense pressure to secure admission to a prestigious university.

Stress Factors: Competition, high expectations, exam stress, academic workload

Impact: Arjun experienced severe anxiety and panic attacks due to the fear of failing to meet his and his parents' expectations. He suffered from insomnia and frequent headaches, which affected his academic performance.

Intervention: Arjun worked with a school counsellor to develop stress management techniques and better time management skills. His school implemented mental health workshops and support groups, which helped Arjun and his peers cope with academic pressure.

Case Study 3: Social Media and Digital Stress

Name: Emily Johnson

Background: Emily is a 22-year-old university student from New York City who is highly active on social media platforms.

Stress Factors: Comparison, FOMO, cyberbullying

Impact: Constant exposure to her peers' curated lives led to feelings of inadequacy and anxiety. Emily also faced cyberbullying, which significantly impacted her self-esteem and mental health.

Intervention: Emily reduced her social media use and focused on positive interactions online. She sought counselling and joined a support group for victims of cyberbullying, which helped her regain confidence and improve her mental health.

Case Study 4: Economic and Financial Stress

Name: Mark Wilson

Background: Mark is a 40-year-old factory worker from Detroit who lost his job during an economic downturn.

Stress Factors: Unemployment, financial instability, debt

Impact: The sudden loss of income and mounting debt led to severe anxiety and depression. Mark struggled to meet basic needs and support his family, which worsened his mental health.

Intervention: Mark received support from a local non-profit organization that provided financial counselling and job placement services. He secured a new job and developed a manageable debt repayment plan, gradually improving his financial situation and mental well-being.

Case Study 5: Personal Expectations and Perfectionism

Name: Jessica Miller

Background: Jessica is a 30-year-old lawyer from Boston with a history of setting high personal standards.

Stress Factors: Unrealistic personal standards, fear of failure, self-criticism

Impact: Jessica's perfectionism led to chronic anxiety and burnout, affecting her work performance and personal life. She often felt paralyzed by the fear of making mistakes.

Intervention: Jessica sought therapy, where she learned to set more realistic goals and practice self-compassion. She gradually reduced her stress levels and improved her overall well-being by changing her mindset.

Case Study 6: Relationship Stress

Name: David Smith

Background: David is a 45-year-old engineer from Chicago experiencing marital conflicts and strained relationships with his teenage children.

Stress Factors: Family dynamics, marital issues, social relationships, peer pressure

Impact: Constant arguments at home affected David's work performance and overall mental health. He felt overwhelmed by the stress from his familial relationships.

Intervention: David and his family attended family therapy, where they learned effective communication and conflict-resolution techniques. Through therapy, they addressed underlying issues and improved their relationships, significantly reducing stress.

Chapter Summary

- Workplace Stress: High job demands, tight deadlines, job insecurity, and lack of control.
- Academic Pressure: Competition, high expectations, exam stress, and heavy workload.
- Social Media and Digital Stress: Comparison, fear of missing out (FOMO), cyberbullying, and online harassment.
- Economic and Financial Stress: Unemployment, financial instability, debt, and financial obligations.
- Personal Expectations and Perfectionism: High personal standards, fear of failure, and self-criticism.
- Relationship Stress: Family dynamics, marital issues, social relationships, and peer pressure.
- Health and Lifestyle Factors: Chronic illness, health anxiety, poor lifestyle choices (diet, exercise, sleep).

CHAPTER THREE

The Effects of Mental Pressure

In this chapter, we will explore the wide-ranging effects of mental pressure on health and productivity. By understanding these effects, you can better recognize the signs of stress in your own life and take steps to mitigate its impact. We will delve into the physical, mental, and behavioural health impacts of stress, supported by scientific research and personal anecdotes. Additionally, we will examine how stress affects productivity in the workplace, academic settings, and personal life. This comprehensive approach will provide you with a deeper understanding of how mental pressure influences various aspects of your life.

Importance of Understanding the Effects of Mental Pressure

Recognizing the effects of mental pressure is crucial for several reasons. First, it enables individuals to identify stress-related symptoms early and seek appropriate interventions. Understanding the physical health impacts, such as cardiovascular issues, immune system suppression, and gastrointestinal problems, can prompt timely medical consultation and lifestyle adjustments. Moreover, awareness of the mental health consequences, including anxiety, depression, and cognitive decline, underscores the importance of mental health care and stress management techniques. Finally, acknowledging the productivity effects of stress, such as decreased efficiency and increased absenteeism, can lead to the implementation of supportive workplace and academic policies. By comprehensively understanding the impacts of mental pressure, you can adopt more effective strategies to enhance your well-being and performance.

Health Impacts

Physical Health Impacts

Cardiovascular Issues

Mental pressure significantly impacts cardiovascular health. Chronic stress triggers the body's fight-or-flight response, leading to the release of stress hormones such as adrenaline and cortisol. These hormones increase heart rate and blood pressure, preparing the body to handle immediate threats. However, prolonged exposure to stress hormones can damage the cardiovascular system. According to the American Heart Association, chronic stress is a major risk factor for hypertension, heart attacks, and strokes. Stress-induced behaviours, such as smoking, overeating, and lack of exercise, further exacerbate cardiovascular risks. Managing stress through relaxation techniques, regular physical activity, and a healthy diet is essential for maintaining heart health.

Immune System Suppression

Chronic stress also suppresses the immune system, making the body more susceptible to infections and diseases. The continuous release of cortisol inhibits the production of cytokines, which are crucial for immune response. A study published in Psychological Bulletin found that individuals under chronic stress exhibit lower levels of immune cell activity, reducing their ability to fight off illnesses. This weakened immune response increases the risk of infections, prolongs recovery times, and can exacerbate chronic illnesses. Stress management practices, such as mindfulness, adequate sleep, and social support, can help bolster the immune system and improve overall health.

Gastrointestinal Problems

The gut-brain connection highlights how mental pressure can manifest in gastrointestinal issues. Stress can disrupt the digestive system, leading to problems such as irritable bowel syndrome (IBS), acid reflux, and ulcers. The gut contains a network of neurons known as the enteric nervous system, which communicates with the central nervous system. Chronic stress can alter this communication, affecting gut motility and enzyme production. Research published in Gastroenterology shows that stress can exacerbate symptoms of IBS, causing abdominal pain, bloating, and changes in bowel habits. Incorporating stress reduction techniques, such as deep breathing exercises, regular physical activity, and a balanced diet, can help alleviate gastrointestinal symptoms.

Personal Anecdote: Example of Physical Health Impact

George Orwell, the famous author, faced severe stress due to his demanding writing career and the political climate of his time. He suffered from chronic lung issues, exacerbated by the stress of constant deadlines and the pressures of his work. Despite his health problems, Orwell continued to work tirelessly, but his stress undoubtedly impacted his overall health and well-being. This example illustrates how mental pressure can significantly affect physical health, even in individuals known for their resilience and productivity.

Mental Health Impacts

Anxiety and Depression

Mental pressure is a significant contributor to anxiety and depression. Chronic stress activates the body's stress response, leading to prolonged exposure to stress hormones like cortisol. Over time, this hormonal imbalance can alter brain function, particularly in areas related to mood regulation such as the amygdala and prefrontal cortex. According to the National Institute of Mental Health (NIMH), individuals under chronic stress are at a higher risk of developing anxiety disorders and major depressive disorder.

Anxiety manifests as persistent worry, tension, and a sense of impending doom. Physical symptoms often accompany these feelings, including increased heart rate, sweating, and tremors. Depression, on the other hand, is characterized by persistent sadness, loss of interest in activities, and feelings of hopelessness. Both conditions can significantly impair daily functioning and quality of life. A study published in The Lancet Psychiatry highlighted that chronic stress is a major predictor of anxiety and depression, emphasizing the need for effective stress management strategies to prevent these mental health issues.

Cognitive Decline

Chronic stress can lead to cognitive decline by affecting the structure and function of the brain. The hippocampus, a critical area for learning and memory, is particularly vulnerable to the effects of stress. Research published in The Journal of Neuroscience indicates that prolonged exposure to high levels of cortisol can reduce neurogenesis (the formation of new neurons) in the hippocampus, leading to memory impairments and difficulties in learning.

Furthermore, stress can impair executive functions such as decision-making, problem-solving, and attention. This is because stress affects the prefrontal cortex, the brain region responsible for these higher-order cognitive processes. Individuals under chronic stress often report issues with concentration, forgetfulness, and reduced cognitive flexibility, making it challenging to navigate daily tasks and complex problems.

Sleep Disturbances

Sleep disturbances are a common consequence of mental pressure. Stress can lead to insomnia, characterized by difficulty falling asleep, staying asleep, or waking up too early. The anxiety associated with stress often leads to a heightened state of arousal, making it hard for individuals to relax and fall asleep. Additionally, stress can disrupt the sleep cycle, leading to poor sleep quality and frequent awakenings.

A study published in the Journal of Clinical Sleep Medicine found that individuals experiencing high levels of stress are more likely to suffer from sleep disorders, including insomnia and sleep apnea. Poor sleep further exacerbates stress, creating a vicious cycle that can be difficult to break. Effective stress management techniques, such as mindfulness meditation and cognitive-behavioural therapy for insomnia (CBT-I), are essential for improving sleep quality and overall well-being.

Personal Anecdote: Example of Mental Health Impact

Tina Turner, the legendary singer, faced immense stress due to her tumultuous personal life and demanding career. She publicly shared her struggles with depression and anxiety, highlighting how the pressures of her profession and personal challenges affected her mental health. Turner's openness about seeking therapy and practicing mindfulness techniques underscored the importance of addressing mental pressure to maintain mental health and resilience. Her journey serves as an inspiration for others dealing with similar struggles.

Behavioral Health Impacts

Substance Abuse

Substance abuse is a common but harmful way individuals cope with mental pressure. Under chronic stress, individuals may turn to alcohol, drugs, or other substances as a form of self-medication to alleviate their stress symptoms. While these substances may provide temporary relief, they often lead to dependency and worsen the overall mental and physical health.

The Substance Abuse and Mental Health Services Administration (SAMHSA) reports that people experiencing high levels of stress are significantly more likely to engage in substance abuse. This behaviour can lead to a vicious cycle, where substance use exacerbates stress symptoms, leading to increased dependency and higher levels of stress.

Eating Disorders

Mental pressure can also contribute to the development of eating disorders, such as anorexia nervosa, bulimia nervosa, and binge eating disorder. Stress can trigger unhealthy eating behaviours as individuals attempt to gain control over their stress through food. For some, this may involve restrictive eating or excessive dieting, while others may turn to binge eating as a coping mechanism.

A study published in The American Journal of Clinical Nutrition found a strong correlation between stress and disordered eating behaviours. The study emphasized the importance of addressing underlying stress to prevent and treat eating disorders. Interventions such as therapy, nutritional counselling, and stress management techniques can help individuals develop healthier relationships with food and their bodies.

Risky Behaviors

Chronic stress can lead to an increase in risky behaviours as individuals seek to escape or mitigate their stress. These behaviours include reckless driving, unsafe sexual practices, and impulsive decision-making. Stress impairs judgment and increases the likelihood of taking risks without fully considering the consequences.

A study published in Psychological Science found that individuals under significant stress are more prone to engage in risky behaviours due to impaired cognitive control and emotional regulation. This can result in accidents, injuries, and long-term negative impacts on health and well-being. Effective stress management can help mitigate these behaviours by improving emotional regulation and decision-making abilities.

Personal Anecdote: Example of Behavioral Health Impact

Amy Winehouse, the talented singer, struggled with substance abuse throughout her career. The intense pressure of fame and personal issues led her to rely heavily on drugs and alcohol as coping mechanisms. Despite her immense talent, Winehouse's battles with addiction ultimately overshadowed her career and contributed to her untimely death. Her story serves as a cautionary tale about the dangers of using substances to cope with mental pressure and the importance of seeking healthy, constructive ways to manage stress.

Chapter Summary

- Physical Health Impacts: Stress-related issues like cardiovascular problems, immune system suppression, and gastrointestinal issues.

- Mental Health Impacts: Increased risk of anxiety, depression, and cognitive decline.
- Behavioral Health Impacts: Higher likelihood of substance abuse, eating disorders, and risky behaviours.
- Workplace Productivity: Reduced efficiency, increased absenteeism, and higher burnout and turnover rates.
- Academic Performance: Decreased concentration and memory, lower grades, and higher dropout rates.
- Personal Life Productivity: Impact on daily routines, relationship strain, and decreased motivation for personal goals.

CHAPTER FOUR

IDENTIFYING YOUR TRIGGERS

This chapter focuses on identifying the triggers that lead to mental pressure. By understanding what triggers stress, individuals can take proactive steps to manage their reactions and reduce overall stress levels. Identifying triggers is the first step in developing effective coping strategies, which can significantly improve one's quality of life.

Importance of Identifying Personal Triggers Recognizing personal triggers is crucial for effective stress management. Knowing what causes stress can help individuals avoid or mitigate these triggers, leading to improved mental health and well-being. By identifying specific stressors, individuals can develop targeted strategies to address them, enhancing their ability to handle stress and maintain emotional balance.

Personal Anecdote: My School Experience with Triggers of Pressure When I was in school, numerous factors triggered my stress, from academic expectations to social dynamics. These pressures often felt overwhelming and impacted my performance and mental health. For instance, the pressure to excel in exams and the fear of not meeting my parents' expectations were constant sources of anxiety. Additionally, navigating social relationships and dealing with peer pressure added to my stress. By identifying and understanding these triggers, I was able to develop strategies to manage them effectively, such as setting realistic goals, seeking support from teachers and friends, and practicing relaxation techniques. This personal journey highlights the importance of recognizing and addressing stress triggers to improve overall well-being.

Understanding Triggers

Definition of Triggers Triggers are specific events, situations, or thoughts that provoke a stress response. These can be external, such as environmental factors, or internal, such as cognitive and emotional processes. External triggers might include work deadlines, financial pressures, or social conflicts, while internal triggers can involve negative self-talk, unrealistic expectations, or unresolved emotional issues.

How Triggers Impact Mental Pressure When a trigger is encountered, it activates the body's stress response, which can lead to a variety of physical and emotional reactions. Physically, the body might respond with increased heart rate, muscle tension, and the release of stress hormones like cortisol and adrenaline. Emotionally, triggers can cause feelings of anxiety, fear, frustration, or sadness. These reactions can impair cognitive functions, reduce concentration, and affect decision-making abilities. Recognizing these triggers is the first step in managing stress effectively, as it allows individuals to identify patterns and develop strategies to cope with or avoid these stressors.

The Role of Awareness in Managing Stress Awareness of stress triggers allows individuals to anticipate and prepare for stressful situations, reducing their overall impact. Mindfulness and self-awareness are crucial tools in this process. By practicing mindfulness, individuals can stay present and recognize their immediate reactions to stressors without judgment. This heightened awareness helps in identifying the specific events or thoughts that trigger stress, making it easier to address them. For example, if an individual notices that public speaking consistently triggers anxiety, they can take steps to prepare more thoroughly, practice relaxation techniques beforehand, or seek professional support to build confidence. The ability to anticipate stressors and implement coping strategies can significantly reduce the overall impact of stress on one's life.

Work-Related Triggers

High Job Demands and Deadlines

Stress from excessive workloads and tight deadlines is a common issue in many workplaces. When employees are required to handle more tasks than they can manage within a given timeframe, it can lead to significant mental pressure. This stress often manifests in the form of frequent overtime, an inability to complete tasks efficiently, and a constant feeling of being overwhelmed. The pressure to meet tight deadlines can result in anxiety, burnout, and decreased job satisfaction. Employees may feel that no matter how hard they work, they can never catch up, leading to a sense of perpetual stress.

Signs to Recognize This Trigger

1. Frequent overtime and long working hours
2. Inability to complete tasks within deadlines
3. Constant feelings of being overwhelmed and rushed
4. Increased anxiety and burnout

Lack of Control and Autonomy

A lack of control and autonomy over one's work can also be a significant stressor. When employees have little say in how they perform their tasks or are micromanaged by supervisors, it can lead to feelings of powerlessness and frustration. This stress is particularly common in environments where employees are not given the opportunity to make decisions or contribute ideas. The lack of autonomy can stifle creativity and motivation, leading to disengagement and dissatisfaction with work. Over time, this can result in a decline in mental health, as the constant feeling of being controlled erodes self-esteem and increases stress levels.

Signs to Recognize This Trigger

1. Feeling powerless and unable to influence work decisions
2. Micromanagement by supervisors
3. Lack of opportunities to contribute ideas or make decisions
4. Decreased motivation and job satisfaction

Interpersonal Conflicts and Workplace Bullying

Interpersonal conflicts and workplace bullying are severe stressors that can significantly impact an individual's mental health. Conflicts with colleagues or supervisors can create a hostile work environment, leading to stress and anxiety. Workplace bullying, which includes behaviours such as intimidation, harassment, and verbal abuse, can have devastating effects on an employee's well-being. These negative interactions can lead to a dread of going to work, decreased productivity, and a higher risk of mental health issues such as depression and anxiety. It is crucial to recognize these signs early and address the underlying issues to prevent long-term damage.

Signs to Recognize This Trigger

1. Dread of going to work and negative feelings about the workplace
2. Frequent negative interactions with colleagues or supervisors
3. Signs of harassment or bullying, such as intimidation or verbal abuse
4. Decreased productivity and job satisfaction

Case Study: Example of Work-Related Triggers

John, a project manager at a tech firm, faced high job demands and tight deadlines, which led to frequent overtime and burnout. Additionally, he experienced workplace bullying from a supervisor who constantly micromanaged and criticized his work. These stressors made John dread going to work and negatively impacted his mental health. Seeking help, John reported the bullying to HR and began setting boundaries to manage his workload better. He also practiced stress-relief techniques such as mindfulness and exercise. With support from his company and a commitment to self-care, John was able to manage his stress and improve his work environment.

Personal and Social Triggers

Family Dynamics and Expectations

Family dynamics and expectations can be significant sources of stress. Pressure to meet familial standards, whether related to career, education, or personal behaviour, can create a constant feeling of inadequacy and anxiety. Conflicts within the family, such as disagreements between parents and children or tensions between siblings, can further exacerbate stress levels.

The emotional toll of trying to satisfy everyone's expectations can lead to mental exhaustion and decreased self-esteem. This stress often manifests in physical symptoms such as headaches and fatigue, and can also cause emotional issues like irritability and depression.

Signs to Recognize This Trigger

1. Feeling constant pressure to meet family expectations
2. Frequent conflicts or arguments at home
3. Physical symptoms such as headaches and fatigue linked to family stress
4. Emotional issues like irritability, anxiety, and depression due to family dynamics

Social Relationships and Peer Pressure

Social interactions and peer pressure are common sources of stress, especially among adolescents and young adults. The desire to fit in and be accepted by peers can lead individuals to conform to behaviours and values that may not align with their own. This pressure to conform can cause significant stress and anxiety, particularly in social settings where the fear of judgment is high. Social media exacerbates these feelings by constantly showcasing curated and often unrealistic images of others' lives, leading to comparison and self-doubt. Social anxiety can result from these pressures, impacting one's ability to form and maintain healthy relationships.

Signs to Recognize This Trigger

1. Feeling the need to conform to peer behaviours and values
2. Anxiety and stress in social situations
3. Comparing oneself negatively to others, especially on social media
4. Difficulty forming and maintaining healthy relationships

Financial Instability and Responsibilities

Financial instability and responsibilities are major stressors that can have far-reaching impacts on mental health. Constant worry about money, managing debt, and meeting financial obligations can create a pervasive sense of insecurity and stress. This stress is often compounded by the responsibility of providing for oneself or a family, leading to feelings of overwhelm and despair. Financial stress can affect all aspects of life, from daily decision-making to long-term planning, and can lead to serious mental health issues like anxiety and depression. Recognizing financial stress early is crucial for taking steps to manage and alleviate its impact.

Signs to Recognize This Trigger

1. Constant worry about money and financial security
2. Difficulty meeting financial obligations and managing debt
3. Feelings of overwhelm and despair related to financial responsibilities
4. Mental health issues such as anxiety and depression linked to financial stress

Case Study: Example of Personal and Social Triggers

Maria, a single mother of two, faced immense stress from family expectations and financial responsibilities. Her family expected her to maintain a certain standard of living and be the primary caregiver, which created constant pressure. Financial instability added to her stress, as she struggled to make ends meet. Maria managed her stress by seeking support from a financial advisor to better manage her finances and joining a support group for single parents. She also communicated her boundaries and needs to her family, reducing some of the pressure to meet their expectations. These steps helped Maria regain control and improve her well-being.

Self-Assessment Tools and Exercises

Daily Stress Diary

How to Keep a Stress Diary

Maintaining a daily stress diary involves recording your stressors and their impact on your mental and physical well-being. This practice helps identify patterns in stress triggers and develop effective coping strategies. Here are some steps to keep a stress diary:

1. Choose a Format: Use a physical notebook, a digital document, or a stress diary app.
2. Set a Routine: Dedicate a specific time each day to record your stress experiences, preferably at the end of the day.
3. Record Details: Note the date, time, and specific details of the stressor.
4. Describe Your Reaction: Write about your physical and emotional responses to the stressor.
5. Identify Coping Strategies: Document any coping mechanisms you used and their effectiveness.

Example of a Stress Diary Entry

1. Date: June 1, 2024
2. Time: 3:00 PM
3. Stressor: Received a critical email from my boss about a project.
4. Physical Reaction: Heart rate increased, and felt sweaty and tense.
5. Emotional Reaction: Felt anxious, and worried about job security.
6. Coping Strategy: Took a 10-minute walk to clear my mind, and practiced deep breathing.
7. Effectiveness: Felt calmer after the walk, but anxiety lingered.

Benefits of Tracking Stress Triggers

Tracking stress triggers helps in identifying patterns and understanding the root causes of stress. By maintaining a stress diary, you can:

1. **Recognize Patterns:** Notice recurring stressors and understand their frequency and intensity.
2. **Develop Coping Strategies:** Identify which coping mechanisms work best for you.
3. **Improve Self-Awareness:** Gain insights into how stress affects you and your responses to different stressors.
4. **Enhance Communication:** Use your diary entries to communicate with healthcare providers or therapists for better support.

Trigger Mapping Exercise

Step-by-Step Guide to Mapping Your Triggers

Trigger mapping involves creating a visual representation of your stressors and their impacts. Here's how to do it:

1. List Your Stressors: Write down all known stress triggers.
2. Categorize Stressors: Group them into categories such as work, family, social, financial, etc.
3. Identify Reactions: For each stressor, note your physical, emotional, and behavioural reactions.
4. Draw the Map: Create a visual map with stressors as nodes and reactions branching out from each node.
5. Analyze Patterns: Look for connections and patterns among different stressors and reactions.

Visual Representation of Triggers and Their Impact

Example 1: A mind map with "Work Stress" in the centre, branching out to "Deadlines," "Lack of Control," and "Conflicts." Further branches show reactions like "Anxiety," "Headaches," and "Insomnia."

Example 2: A flowchart starting with "Financial Stress" leading to "Worry," which splits into "Overeating," "Insomnia," and "Irritability."

Using the Map to Develop Coping Strategies

Once your trigger map is complete, use it to develop personalized stress management plans:

1. Prioritize Stressors: Identify the most frequent or severe stressors to address first.
2. Develop Specific Strategies: Create targeted strategies for each stressor, such as time management for deadlines or assertiveness training for conflicts.

3. Track Progress: Regularly update your map to reflect changes and improvements.

Reflection and Mindfulness Exercises

Techniques for Mindful Reflection on Stress Triggers

Mindful reflection involves being present and non-judgmental about your stress experiences. Techniques include:

1. Daily Reflection: Set aside time each day to reflect on your stressors and responses.
2. Journaling: Write about your thoughts and feelings regarding stress triggers.
3. Meditation: Practice mindfulness meditation to observe your thoughts and reactions without judgment.

Guided Mindfulness Exercises to Increase Awareness

Body Scan: Lie down in a comfortable position. Close your eyes and take a few deep breaths. Slowly bring your attention to your feet, noticing any sensations. Gradually move your attention up your body, part by part, until you reach your head.

Breathing Exercise: Sit comfortably and close your eyes. Focus on your breath. Inhale deeply through your nose, hold for a few seconds, and exhale slowly through your mouth. Repeat for 5-10 minutes, staying present with each breath.

Mindful Observation: Choose an object in your environment. Observe it closely for a few minutes, noting its colour, texture, shape, and any other details. This exercise helps bring your focus to the present moment.

Case Study: Success Story Using Mindfulness for Trigger Identification Lisa, a marketing executive, struggled with work-related stress and frequent anxiety attacks. She started practicing mindfulness meditation daily, focusing on her breath and body sensations. Over time, Lisa became more aware of her stress triggers, such as tight deadlines and critical feedback.

By identifying these triggers, she developed strategies like setting realistic goals and seeking constructive feedback. Mindfulness helped Lisa manage her reactions and reduce the frequency of anxiety attacks, significantly improving her mental well-being.

Interactive Elements

Self-Assessment Exercise

Take a moment to reflect on your personal stress triggers by answering the following questions:

1. What situations cause you the most stress? Identify specific scenarios or interactions that consistently make you feel stressed.
2. How do you usually react to these stressors? Consider your physical, emotional, and behavioural responses when you face these stressors.
3. What common patterns do you notice in your stress triggers? Look for recurring themes or circumstances that regularly contribute to your stress.

Answering these questions can provide valuable insights into the sources of your stress and how they affect you.

Reflective Questions

1. Which stress triggers can you reduce or eliminate? Think about ways to avoid or minimize exposure to certain stressors.
2. How can you adjust your reactions to unavoidable stress triggers? Explore techniques for changing your response to stressors that you can't avoid, such as practicing relaxation exercises or seeking support.

These reflective questions can help you develop strategies for managing stress more effectively and improving your overall well-being.

Chapter Summary

- Importance of Identifying Personal Triggers: Understanding triggers is crucial for effective stress management.
- Work-Related Triggers: High job demands, lack of control, and interpersonal conflicts.
- Self-Assessment Tools and Exercises: Daily stress diary, trigger mapping, and reflection exercises.
- Health and Lifestyle Triggers: Chronic illness, poor lifestyle choices (diet, exercise, sleep).
- Cognitive and Emotional Triggers: Negative thinking patterns, anxiety, emotional regulation challenges.

CHAPTER FIVE

DEVELOPING HEALTHY COPING MECHANISMS

This chapter focuses on strategies for managing and reducing mental pressure. By adopting healthy coping mechanisms, individuals can improve their resilience and overall well-being. We will explore various techniques and practices that can help manage stress effectively and promote a balanced lifestyle.

Importance of Adopting Healthy Coping Mechanisms

Adopting healthy coping mechanisms is essential for maintaining mental and physical health. These strategies help individuals handle stress more effectively, preventing it from becoming overwhelming. Healthy coping mechanisms can improve emotional regulation, enhance problem-solving skills, and provide a sense of control over one's life. They are crucial for preventing burnout and promoting long-term well-being.

Importance of Self-Care and Mindfulness Practices

Role of Self-Care in Maintaining Mental Health Self-care involves taking intentional actions to care for one's physical, mental, and emotional health. It is a proactive approach to maintaining well-being and preventing stress. Regular self-care practices can boost mood, increase energy levels, and improve overall quality of life. It helps in creating a balanced routine that includes rest, relaxation, and activities that bring joy and fulfilment.

Benefits of Mindfulness Practices for Stress Reduction Mindfulness involves being fully present in the moment without judgment. It helps individuals become more aware of their thoughts, feelings, and physical sensations, which can reduce the impact of stress. Practicing mindfulness regularly can lead to reduced anxiety, improved focus, and enhanced emotional resilience. It allows individuals to respond to stressors more calmly and effectively.

Physical Activity and Exercise

Benefits of Physical Activity

Engaging in regular physical activity offers numerous benefits for mental and physical health. One of the primary advantages is its ability to reduce stress hormones, such as cortisol and adrenaline, which help to alleviate feelings of stress and anxiety. Exercise also stimulates the production of endorphins, which are natural mood lifters. These chemicals in the brain help to foster a sense of well-being and relaxation.

Physical activity can significantly improve mood and energy levels. By increasing the flow of oxygen and nutrients to tissues, exercise enhances cardiovascular health, boosts stamina, and increases overall energy. Regular physical activity can also improve sleep quality, which is essential for stress management and overall health.

Types of Exercise

Aerobic Exercises Aerobic exercises are activities that increase your heart rate and improve cardiovascular fitness. Examples include running, cycling, swimming, and brisk walking. These exercises help to burn calories, improve heart health, and elevate mood through the release of endorphins.

Strength Training Strength training involves exercises that improve muscle strength and endurance. This can include weightlifting, using resistance bands, or body-weight exercises like push-ups and squats. Strength training helps to build and maintain muscle mass, improve bone density, and boost metabolism. It also enhances self-esteem and confidence through the achievement of physical fitness goals.

Flexibility and Balance Exercises that focus on flexibility and balance, such as yoga and Pilates, are excellent for reducing stress. These activities promote relaxation, improve posture, and enhance body awareness. Yoga, in particular, combines physical movement with breath control and meditation, making it a powerful tool for reducing anxiety and improving mental clarity.

Actionable Steps

Create a Weekly Exercise Plan Developing a structured exercise plan can help ensure consistency and variety in your workouts. Start by setting realistic goals and scheduling exercise sessions into your weekly routine. Aim for at least 150 minutes of moderate aerobic activity or 75 minutes of vigorous activity per week, along with two or more days of strength training.

Start with Short, Manageable Workouts and Gradually Increase Intensity you are new to exercise or have been inactive for a while, begin with short, manageable workouts. Start with 10-15 minute sessions and gradually increase the duration and intensity as your fitness improves. This approach helps prevent injury and ensures that you stay motivated as you progress.

Join a Fitness Class or Find an Exercise Buddy for Motivation Participating in a fitness class or finding an exercise buddy can provide additional motivation and accountability. Group classes offer a social component that can make workouts more enjoyable and less intimidating. Having a workout partner can also provide encouragement, making it easier to stay committed to your exercise routine.

Time Management and Organization

Benefits of Effective Time Management

Effective time management is crucial for reducing feelings of overwhelm and increasing productivity. When you manage your time well, you can prioritize tasks, handle your workload more efficiently, and create a better work-life balance. This leads to reduced stress levels and a greater sense of control over your day-to-day activities.

Reduces Feelings of Overwhelm and Increases Productivity By organizing tasks and setting priorities, effective time management helps to break down large projects into manageable steps. This approach minimizes the feelings of being overwhelmed by large tasks and improves overall productivity. When tasks are well-organized and time is allocated efficiently, it becomes easier to complete projects on time and with less stress.

Helps Prioritize Tasks and Manage Workload Time management techniques enable you to identify and focus on the most important tasks. Prioritizing your workload ensures that critical tasks are addressed first, reducing the likelihood of last-minute rushes and missed deadlines. This not only enhances your efficiency but also improves the quality of your work by allowing adequate time for each task.

Techniques for Better Time Management

Prioritization Methods

Eisenhower Matrix: This method helps you categorize tasks into four quadrants based on their urgency and importance. Tasks are divided into:

1. Urgent and important
2. Important but not urgent
3. Urgent but not important

Neither urgent nor important This matrix allows you to focus on high-priority tasks and delegate or eliminate low-priority ones.

ABC Method: This technique involves categorizing tasks into three groups:

1. A: High-priority tasks that are critical to your goals
2. B: Important tasks that are not as urgent as A tasks
3. C: Low-priority tasks that have minimal consequences if delayed By organizing tasks this way, you can tackle the most crucial ones first.

Use of Planners and Digital Tools Using planners or digital tools can streamline your time management process. Planners help you visualize your schedule, set deadlines, and track your progress. Digital tools, such as calendar apps and project management software, offer additional features like reminders, task lists, and collaboration capabilities, making it easier to stay organized and on track.

Actionable Steps

Create Daily and Weekly Schedules Developing a routine by creating daily and weekly schedules helps you allocate specific times for various tasks. Start each day by listing the tasks you need to complete and prioritize them based on importance and deadlines. Plan your week in advance to ensure a balanced distribution of work and leisure activities.

Set Realistic Goals and Break Tasks into Smaller Steps Setting achievable goals is essential for maintaining motivation and avoiding burnout. Break down large tasks into smaller, more manageable steps. This not only makes the tasks less daunting but also provides a sense of accomplishment as you complete each step.

Allocate Specific Times for Work, Rest, and Leisure Activities It's important to allocate time for rest and leisure activities to maintain a healthy work-life balance. Schedule specific times for work-related tasks, breaks, exercise, and hobbies. Ensuring that you have time to relax and recharge can improve your overall productivity and well-being.

Effective time management is a powerful tool for reducing stress and increasing productivity. By implementing prioritization methods, using planners and digital tools, and following actionable steps, you can manage your workload more efficiently and create a balanced, productive lifestyle.

Social Support and Connection

Importance of Social Support

Social support plays a crucial role in managing stress and maintaining mental well-being. It provides both emotional comfort and practical help, which are essential for navigating life's challenges.

Provides Emotional Comfort and Practical Having a strong social support network means having people to turn to during difficult times. Friends, family, and colleagues can offer a listening ear, share advice, and encourage. This emotional support helps alleviate stress and fosters a sense of belonging. Practical help, such as assistance with tasks or sharing resources, can also lighten your load, making it easier to manage daily responsibilities.

Strengthens Resilience and Reduces Feelings of Isolation Social connections enhance resilience by providing a buffer against stress. Knowing that you have people who care about you and are willing to help can make stressful situations feel more manageable. Additionally, social interactions reduce feelings of isolation and loneliness, which can exacerbate stress and negatively impact mental health.

Building a Support Network

Cultivating Relationships with Family, Friends, and Colleagues Investing time and effort into building strong relationships with family, friends, and colleagues is essential. Regular communication, mutual support, and shared experiences strengthen these bonds. Make an effort to reach out, stay connected, and show appreciation for those in your life.

Joining Support Groups or Clubs with Shared Interests Engaging with support groups or clubs that share your interests can expand your social network and provide additional layers of support. Whether it's a hobby group, a professional organization, or a community support group, these connections can offer valuable perspectives, shared experiences, and a sense of community.

Actionable Steps

Schedule Regular Social Activities Incorporate regular social activities into your routine to maintain and strengthen your relationships. This could be weekly family dinners, monthly outings with friends, or casual meetups with colleagues. Consistent interaction helps keep your support network robust and active.

Reach Out to Others When Feeling Stressed Don't hesitate to reach out to your support network when you're feeling overwhelmed. A simple conversation can provide relief and perspective. Sharing your concerns with someone you trust can lighten your emotional burden and help you gain clarity on how to address your stressors.

Be Open to Giving and Receiving Support Effective social support is a two-way street. Be willing to offer help to others in your network, whether it's through listening, sharing advice, or providing practical assistance. At the same time, be open to receiving support from others. Accepting help is not a sign of weakness; it's a crucial part of maintaining a healthy, balanced life.

Incorporating social support and connection into your life is a powerful way to manage stress and enhance well-being. you can significantly improve your resilience and reduce feelings of isolation. These actionable steps provide a practical framework for leveraging the power of social connections to navigate life's challenges more effectively.

Relaxation Techniques and Hobbies

Value of Relaxation and Leisure

Relaxation and leisure are crucial for recharging and maintaining balance. They help you step back, relax, and reset, which boosts creativity and enjoyment in life.

Types of Relaxation Techniques

Deep Breathing Deep breathing calms your mind and reduces stress. It's simple: inhale deeply, hold for a few seconds, and exhale slowly.

Progressive Muscle Relaxation This technique involves tensing and then relaxing each muscle group. It helps reduce physical tension and stress.

Guided Imagery Guided imagery uses visualization to create a sense of peace and relaxation. Imagine a serene scene and focus on the details to calm your mind.

Actionable Steps

Incorporate Relaxation Techniques into Your Daily Routine Make relaxation a habit. Set aside a few minutes each day for deep breathing, muscle relaxation, or guided imagery.

Engage in Hobbies and Activities that Bring Joy and Relaxation Dedicate time to hobbies that you love. Whether it's reading, painting, gardening, or playing an instrument, these activities reduce stress and enhance your quality of life.

Incorporating relaxation techniques and hobbies into your daily routine helps you recharge and maintain balance. Use these simple methods to reduce stress and boost your overall well-being.

Chapter Summary

- Physical Activity and Exercise: Reduces stress hormones, stimulates endorphins, and improves mood and energy levels.
- Time Management and Organization: Reduces overwhelm, increases productivity, and helps prioritize tasks.
- Social Support and Connection: Provides emotional comfort, and practical help, and strengthens resilience.
- Relaxation Techniques and Hobbies: Helps recharge, maintain balance, enhance creativity, and enjoyment of life.

CHAPTER SIX

BUILDING RESILIENCE

Why Resilience Matters

Resilience is your ability to bounce back from adversity, stress, and challenges. Think of it as your mental and emotional flexibility. Just like a rubber band that snaps back into shape after being stretched, resilience allows you to recover quickly from setbacks. This ability to adapt and persevere is crucial in a world that is constantly changing and throwing new challenges your way.

Benefits

Building resilience isn't just about surviving tough times; it's about thriving despite them. When you develop resilience, you strengthen your mental health. It helps reduce anxiety and depression by giving you tools to manage stress more effectively. Resilient people are better at handling life's ups and downs without being overwhelmed by them.

Long-term, resilience leads to greater success. Resilient people are more likely to achieve their goals and maintain strong relationships. They can navigate obstacles with confidence and maintain a positive outlook, even in difficult circumstances. This not only improves their quality of life but also sets them up for sustained success in their personal and professional lives.

"

In essence, resilience is a skill that enhances your overall well-being and equips you to face life's challenges with strength and determination."

What is Resilience?

Definition and Traits of Resilient People

Resilience is the ability to adapt and recover from adversity, stress, and life's inevitable challenges. It's like a mental muscle that you can strengthen over time. Resilient people don't avoid difficulties; they face them head-on and find ways to overcome them.

Here are the key traits of resilient people:

1. **Optimism:** They maintain a positive outlook even in tough times. Optimism doesn't mean ignoring problems; it means believing they can be managed and overcome.
2. **Adaptability:** Resilient people are flexible. They can adjust their plans and strategies when faced with new obstacles or changing circumstances.
3. **Perseverance:** They don't give up easily. When they encounter setbacks, they persist until they find a solution.
4. **Emotional Awareness:** They understand their emotions and use this awareness to handle stress and stay calm under pressure.
5. **Support Networks:** They cultivate strong relationships with family, friends, and colleagues. They know when to seek help and are also there for others.
6. **Problem-Solving Skills:** Resilient individuals are proactive. They identify problems, think critically, and develop effective solutions.

Why Resilience is Key to Handling Life's Challenges

Life is unpredictable. You will face obstacles, setbacks, and failures. Resilience is the key to navigating these challenges effectively. Here's why:

1. **Coping with Stress:** Resilience helps you manage stress more effectively. Instead of being overwhelmed, you can stay focused and calm. This reduces the risk of anxiety and depression.

2. **Quick Recovery:** Resilient people bounce back faster from setbacks. Whether it's a job loss, a personal tragedy, or a failed project, they recover quickly and move forward with renewed determination.

3. **Improved Problem-Solving:** When you're resilient, you approach problems with a clear mind. You're better equipped to think critically and find innovative solutions, rather than being paralyzed by fear or uncertainty.

4. **Better Relationships:** Resilience strengthens your relationships. By maintaining a positive outlook and managing stress effectively, you can support others and build stronger, more meaningful connections.

5. **Enhanced Performance:** Whether in your personal life or career, resilience boosts your performance. You're more likely to take on challenges, set and achieve goals, and maintain high levels of productivity and creativity.

6. **Long-Term Success:** Over time, resilience leads to sustained success. You develop the ability to navigate life's ups and downs, maintaining a steady course towards your long-term goals.

"Resilience is not an innate trait; it's a skill that can be developed. By focusing on building resilience, you equip yourself to handle whatever life throws your way. You become more adaptable, more persistent, and more capable of finding joy and success even in the face of adversity."

Steps to Build Resilience

Positive Mindset

Practice Gratitude

Gratitude is a simple but powerful tool for building a positive mindset. When you focus on what you're thankful for, you shift your attention from what's wrong to what's right. This change in perspective can transform your outlook on life.

How to Practice Gratitude:

1. **Daily Gratitude Journal:** Every day, write down three things you're grateful for. They can be big or small. The key is consistency. Over time, this practice trains your brain to look for the positives.
2. **Express Gratitude to Others:** Take time to thank the people around you. A simple "thank you" can strengthen relationships and increase your own sense of well-being.
3. **Reflect on Positive Experiences:** At the end of each day, think about the good things that happened. This reflection reinforces positive memories and helps you end the day on a high note.

Gratitude isn't just about feeling good; it's about recognizing the good. When you practice gratitude regularly, you build a habit of seeing the positive aspects of your life, which fuels a more optimistic and resilient mindset.

Reframe Negativity

Negative thoughts are inevitable, but how you deal with them makes all the difference. Reframing is a technique that helps you turn negative thoughts into positive ones. It's about changing your perspective to see challenges as opportunities.

How to Reframe Negativity:

1. **Identify Negative Thoughts:** The first step is awareness. Pay attention to your inner dialogue. When you catch yourself thinking negatively, pause and take note.
2. **Challenge Negative Thoughts:** Ask yourself if these thoughts are based on facts or assumptions. Often, negative thoughts are exaggerated or irrational.
3. **Reframe with Positive Alternatives:** Once you've identified and challenged the negative thought, replace it with a positive or neutral alternative. For example, if you think, "I'll never get this right," reframe it to, "I'm learning and improving every day."

Examples of Reframing:

- **Negative Thought**: "I failed at this task."
- **Reframed Thought**: "This is an opportunity to learn and grow.
- "Negative Thought: "I'm terrible at public speaking.
- "**Reframed Thought**: "I'm improving with each experience."

Reframing isn't about ignoring problems. It's about viewing them in a way that's constructive and empowering. By consistently practicing reframing, you can reduce the impact of negative thoughts and develop a more resilient mindset.

Action Steps to Build a Positive Mindset

1. **Start a Gratitude Journal:** Write down three things you're grateful for every day. Reflect on why you appreciate these things and how they positively impact your life.
2. **Practice Gratitude in Relationships:** Make it a habit to thank the people around you. Expressing gratitude strengthens your connections and boosts your mood.
3. **Monitor Your Thoughts:** Pay attention to your inner dialogue.When you notice negative thoughts, challenge and reframe them.
4. **Set Aside Time for Reflection:** At the end of each day, spend a few minutes reflecting on positive experiences and achievements. This practice reinforces a positive mindset.

Emotional Regulation

Use Mindfulness

Mindfulness is the practice of being fully present in the moment, without judgment. It helps you become aware of your thoughts and feelings without being overwhelmed by them. This awareness is crucial for regulating your emotions.

How to Practice Mindfulness:

1. **Start with Short Sessions**: Begin with just 5 minutes a day. Sit quietly, close your eyes, and focus on your breath. When your mind wanders, gently bring it back to your breath.
2. **Use Guided Meditations**: Apps like Headspace or Calm offer guided sessions that can help you get started. These meditations provide structure and support, making it easier to develop a routine.
3. **Practice Mindfulness in Daily Activities**: You don't have to sit still to be mindful. Try paying full attention to everyday activities like eating, walking, or even washing dishes. Notice the sensations, smells, and sounds without distraction.

Mindfulness helps you recognize your emotional responses as they arise. By becoming more aware of your emotions, you can choose how to respond rather than reacting impulsively. This control is key to emotional regulation.

Deep Breathing

Deep breathing is a simple yet powerful technique for managing your emotions. When you're stressed, your breathing becomes shallow and rapid. Deep breathing reverses this response, calming your mind and body.

How to Practice Deep Breathing:

- **Find a Quiet Space:** Sit or lie down in a comfortable position. Close your eyes and relax your shoulders.
- **Inhale Deeply:** Breathe in slowly through your nose, allowing your abdomen to expand. Count to four as you inhale.
- **Hold Your Breath:** Hold your breath for a count of four. This pause helps to calm your mind.
- **Exhale Slowly:** Breathe out slowly through your mouth, counting to six. Let go of all tension as you exhale.
- **Repeat:** Continue this cycle for a few minutes, focusing on the rhythm of your breath.

Benefits of Deep Breathing:

1. **Reduces Stress:** Deep breathing lowers cortisol levels, the body's stress hormone.
2. **Increases Oxygen Flow**: This improves brain function and helps you think more clearly.
3. **Promotes Relaxation**: Deep breathing activates the parasympathetic nervous system, which induces a state of calm.

Action Steps to Enhance Emotional Regulation

Incorporate Mindfulness into Your Routine: Start with 5 minutes of mindfulness meditation each morning. Gradually increase the duration as you become more comfortable.

Use Mindfulness in Stressful Situations: When you feel overwhelmed, take a moment to focus on your breath. This pause can help you respond more calmly.

Practice Deep Breathing Daily: Set aside time each day for deep breathing exercises. This can be especially helpful before bed to promote relaxation.

Create Reminders: Place sticky notes or set phone alarms to remind yourself to practice mindfulness and deep breathing throughout the day.

> *"Mindfulness and deep breathing are powerful tools for emotional regulation. They help you stay grounded, reduce stress, and manage your emotions effectively. By incorporating these practices into your daily routine, you can build greater emotional resilience and navigate life's challenges with calm and clarity."*

Strong Connections

Build Supportive Relationships

Strong relationships are the cornerstone of resilience. They provide emotional support, practical help, and a sense of belonging. Building and maintaining these connections can significantly enhance your ability to handle stress and bounce back from adversity.

How to Build Supportive Relationships:

1. **Invest Time in Relationships:** Quality relationships require time and effort. Make it a priority to spend time with family and friends. Regular check-in, whether it's through a phone call, a meal together, or a simple text message.
2. **Be Present:** When you are with others, be fully present. Put away distractions like your phone and focus on the conversation. Listening actively and showing genuine interest in others strengthens your connections.
3. **Offer Help and Support:** Be there for others when they need you. Offering support not only strengthens your relationships but also builds a reciprocal sense of trust and reliability.
4. **Join Groups or Communities:** Engage in activities that interest you. Whether it's a hobby group, a sports team, or a professional organization, being part of a community provides additional layers of support and connection.
5. **Communicate Openly:** Honest and open communication is key to building trust. Share your thoughts and feelings, and encourage others to do the same.

Benefits of Strong Connections:

- Emotional Support: Having someone to talk to reduces stress and provides comfort during tough times.
- Practical Help: Friends and family can offer practical assistance, whether it's advice, resources, or hands-on help.
- Increased Resilience: A strong support network boosts your confidence and resilience, making it easier to handle challenges.
-

Action Steps to Build Strong Connections

1. **Schedule Regular Social Activities**: Plan weekly or monthly get-togethers with friends and family. Consistent interaction helps maintain strong bonds.
2. **Reach Out Regularly:** Make a habit of reaching out to at least one person each day. A quick call or message can make a big difference in maintaining connections.
3. **Be Open to New Relationships:** Join new groups or try new activities to meet people with similar interests. Expanding your network increases your support base.
4. **Practice Active Listening**: When conversing, focus on understanding the other person's perspective. Show empathy and provide thoughtful responses.

Goal Setting

Set SMART Goals and Celebrate Progress

Setting goals gives you direction and purpose. SMART goals (Specific, Measurable, Achievable, Relevant, Time-bound) provide a clear roadmap for what you want to achieve and how to get there.

How to Set SMART Goals:

1. **Specific:** Define your goal clearly. What exactly do you want to accomplish? The more specific your goal, the easier it is to focus on achieving it.
2. **Measurable:** Determine how you will measure progress. What metrics will you use to track your success? This helps you stay on course and recognize achievements.
3. **Achievable:** Set realistic goals that are within your reach. Consider your current abilities and resources. Setting achievable goals builds confidence and prevents frustration.
4. **Relevant:** Ensure your goals align with your values and long-term objectives. Relevance keeps you motivated and committed.

5. **Time-bound:** Set a deadline for your goal. A clear timeframe creates a sense of urgency and helps prioritize tasks.

Benefits of Setting SMART Goals:

- **Clarity:** Clear goals provide direction and focus.
- **Motivation:** Achieving small milestones along the way boosts motivation.
- **Accountability:** Measurable goals make it easier to hold yourself accountable.

Celebrate Progress: Recognizing and celebrating your achievements, no matter how small, reinforces positive behaviour and keeps you motivated.

How to Celebrate Progress:

1. **Track Milestones:** Keep a journal or use a tracking app to monitor your progress. Celebrate when you reach key milestones.
2. **Reward Yourself:** Treat yourself when you achieve a goal. Rewards can be small, like a favourite treat, or big, like a weekend getaway.
3. **Reflect on Achievements:** Take time to reflect on what you've accomplished. Consider what worked well and how you can apply those strategies to future goals.
4. **Share Success:** Share your achievements with friends or family. Their encouragement and recognition can further boost your motivation.

Action Steps for Goal Setting

1. **Define Your Goals:** Write down your SMART goals and ensure they are specific, measurable, achievable, relevant, and time-bound.
2. **Create an Action Plan:** Break down each goal into smaller, actionable steps. Assign deadlines to each step.

3. **Track Your Progress:** Use a journal, planner, or app to keep track of your progress. Regularly review and adjust your action plan as needed.
4. **Celebrate Milestones:** Acknowledge and celebrate each milestone. Reflect on your achievements and reward yourself for your hard work.

Self-Care

Prioritize Health and Joy

Self-care is about taking deliberate actions to nurture your physical, mental, and emotional well-being. It's essential for maintaining balance and resilience.

How to Prioritize Self-Care:

1. **Maintain a Balanced Diet:** Eat nutritious meals that fuel your body and mind. Proper nutrition supports overall health and energy levels.
2. **Exercise Regularly:** Physical activity reduces stress and boosts mood. Find an exercise routine that you enjoy and stick with it.
3. **Get Adequate Sleep:** Aim for 7-9 hours of quality sleep each night. Good sleep is crucial for mental and physical health.
4. **Engage in Joyful Activities:** Make time for hobbies and activities that bring you joy. Whether it's reading, painting, or spending time outdoors, these activities rejuvenate your spirit.

Benefits of Self-Care:

- Improved Health: Regular self-care practices enhance your physical and mental health.
- Increased Resilience: Taking care of yourself equips you to handle stress and challenges more effectively.
- Greater Happiness: Engaging in activities you love increases your overall happiness and satisfaction.

Action Steps for Self-Care

- **Schedule Self-Care Time**: Set aside specific times each day or week for self-care activities.
- **Listen to Your Body**: Pay attention to your physical and emotional needs. Rest when you're tired and seek help when needed.
- **Incorporate Joyful Activities**: Make a list of activities that bring you joy and incorporate them into your routine.

> *"Prioritizing self-care ensures that you have the energy and resilience to face life's challenges. By focusing on your health and joy, you create a strong foundation for a balanced and fulfilling life."*

Inspirational Stories

Examples of People Overcoming Adversity

Story 1: J.K. Rowling – From Struggling Single Mother to Bestselling Author

J.K. Rowling's journey to becoming one of the most successful authors in history is a testament to resilience and perseverance. Before she wrote the Harry Potter series, Rowling faced numerous challenges. She was a single mother living on welfare, struggling to make ends meet. Despite her difficult circumstances, she pursued her passion for writing.

Rowling wrote the first Harry Potter book while coping with depression and raising her daughter. She faced multiple rejections from publishers before Bloomsbury finally accepted her manuscript. Even then, the initial print run was just 500 copies.

Rowling's resilience paid off. Harry Potter became a global phenomenon, selling over 500 million copies worldwide. Her story is a powerful example of how determination and perseverance can turn adversity into extraordinary success.

Source: Biography of J.K. Rowling

Story 2: Malala Yousafzai – Champion for Girls' Education

Malala Yousafzai's story is one of incredible bravery and resilience. Growing up in Pakistan, Malala was passionate about education, even as the Taliban began restricting girls' access to school. At 15, she was shot in the head by a Taliban gunman for advocating for girls' education.

Despite the life-threatening injury, Malala survived and continued her fight for education. She was flown to the UK for intensive rehabilitation. Instead of being silenced, Malala's voice grew stronger. She co-authored the memoir "I Am Malala" and founded the Malala Fund to support girls' education globally.

In 2014, at age 17, Malala became the youngest-ever Nobel Prize laureate. Her resilience and courage in the face of extreme adversity have inspired millions and brought global attention to the importance of education for all.

Source: Malala Fund

Story 3: Nick Vujicic – Life Without Limbs

Nick Vujicic was born with tetra-amelia syndrome, a rare disorder characterized by the absence of arms and legs. Growing up, Nick faced bullying, depression, and loneliness. At times, he felt hopeless and questioned his purpose in life.

Despite these challenges, Nick developed a resilient mindset. He decided to focus on what he could do rather than what he couldn't. Nick learned to write with his foot, use a computer, and even swim and surf. He found strength in his faith and began to inspire others through motivational speaking.

Today, Nick Vujicic is a renowned speaker and author, sharing his story with millions around the world. He founded the non-profit organization Life Without Limbs, which aims to inspire and encourage people to overcome their own challenges. Nick's story demonstrates that resilience and a positive attitude can help you conquer even the most daunting obstacles.

Source: Life Without Limbs

Story 4: Bethany Hamilton – Overcoming the Odds in Surfing

Bethany Hamilton's life changed dramatically at the age of 13 when she lost her left arm in a shark attack while surfing. A competitive surfer, Bethany's future seemed uncertain after the traumatic incident. However, her resilience and determination were unwavering.

Just one month after the attack, Bethany returned to the water, adapting her technique to surf with one arm. Within two years, she won her first national title. Bethany's comeback story became widely known, inspiring millions.

Bethany continues to compete in surfing at the highest levels, and she uses her platform to motivate others through her foundation, Friends of Bethany. The foundation supports shark attack survivors and amputees. Bethany's story is a powerful example of how resilience can transform tragedy into triumph.

Source: Bethany Hamilton's Official Website

"These real-life stories illustrate the incredible power of resilience. J.K. Rowling, Malala Yousafzai, Nick Vujicic, and Bethany Hamilton each faced severe adversity but refused to be defeated. Their journeys show that with determination, a positive mindset, and unwavering perseverance, it is possible to overcome even the most challenging obstacles and achieve greatness."

Practical Exercises

Daily Practices

Journaling

Journaling is a powerful tool for building resilience. It helps you process emotions, clarify thoughts, and reflect on experiences.

How to Journal:

- Set Aside Time Daily: Dedicate 10-15 minutes each day for journaling. Morning or evening works best for reflection.
- Be Honest: Write about your true feelings and thoughts. This is your private space to express yourself freely.
- Focus on Gratitude and Goals: Start with what you're grateful for and what you want to achieve. This positive focus sets a constructive tone.

Benefits of Journaling:

- **Emotional Clarity:** Helps you understand and manage your emotions.
- **Stress Relief:** Reduces stress by getting worries out of your mind and onto paper.
- **Goal Tracking:** Keeps you focused on your goals and progress.

Meditation

Meditation enhances mindfulness, reducing stress and improving emotional regulation.

How to Meditate:

Find a Quiet Space: Sit comfortably in a quiet area.

Focus on Your Breath: Pay attention to your breathing. Inhale deeply, hold, and exhale slowly.

Stay Present: When your mind wanders, gently bring it back to your breath.

Benefits of Meditation:

Reduces Anxiety: Lowers cortisol levels and calms the mind.

Enhances Focus: Improves concentration and mental clarity.

Emotional Stability: Helps you manage emotions and react calmly.

Affirmations

Affirmations are positive statements that help you overcome negative thoughts and self-doubt.

How to Use Affirmations:

- **Choose Positive Statements:** Select affirmations that resonate with your goals and values.

- **Repeat Daily:** Say them aloud every morning or write them down.
- **Believe in Them:** Conviction is key. Believe in the power of your words.

Examples of Affirmations:

- "I am capable and strong."
- "I handle challenges with grace and ease."
- "Every day, I am becoming more resilient."

Benefits of Affirmations:

- **Boosts Confidence:** Reinforces a positive self-image.
- **Reduces Negative Thoughts:** Replaces negativity with positivity.
- **Increases Motivation:** Keeps you focused on your goals and encourages persistence.

Activities

Team Sports

Team sports build resilience by teaching cooperation, discipline, and perseverance.

How to Get Involved:

Join a Local Team: Look for community leagues or sports clubs.

Commit to Practice: Regular participation enhances skills and teamwork.

Stay Positive: Focus on learning and improvement, not just winning.

Benefits of Team Sports:

Builds Camaraderie: Strengthens social connections and support networks.

Teaches Discipline: Encourages regular practice and commitment.

Enhances Physical Health: Improves fitness and reduces stress.

Volunteering

Volunteering boosts resilience by fostering a sense of purpose and community.

How to Volunteer:

Find a Cause: Choose a cause that you're passionate about.

Schedule Regular Time: Commit to volunteering regularly.

Engage Actively: Be present and proactive in your volunteering efforts.

Benefits of Volunteering:

Sense of Purpose: Provides meaningful engagement and satisfaction.

Community Connection: Builds relationships and a sense of belonging.

Personal Growth: Develop empathy, patience, and problem-solving skills.

Challenging Hobbies

Engaging in challenging hobbies helps you build resilience by pushing your limits and encouraging growth.

How to Start:

Choose a Hobby: Pick something that interests you and poses a challenge.

Set Goals: Establish clear, achievable goals for your hobby.

Practice Regularly: Dedicate time each week to improving your skills.

Examples of Challenging Hobbies:

Rock Climbing: Requires physical strength, mental focus, and problem-solving.

Learning a New Language: Enhances cognitive abilities and perseverance.

Playing a Musical Instrument: Develops discipline, creativity, and patience.

Benefits of Challenging Hobbies:

Builds Confidence: Achieving new skills boosts self-esteem.

Enhances Problem-Solving: Encourages creative thinking and persistence.

Reduces Stress: Provides a productive outlet for stress and anxiety.

Conclusion

Recap the Importance of Resilience

Resilience is your ability to bounce back from adversity, handle stress, and thrive despite challenges. It's not just about surviving; it's about thriving. Building resilience improves your mental health, enhances your problem-solving abilities, and boosts your overall well-being.

Implement These Strategies Daily

Incorporate these practical strategies into your daily routine to strengthen your resilience:

Practice Gratitude: Start a gratitude journal and reflect on the positive aspects of your life.

Reframe Negativity: Challenge negative thoughts and replace them with positive alternatives.

Use Mindfulness and Deep Breathing: Stay present and calm through mindfulness meditation and deep breathing exercises.

Build Strong Connections: Invest time in relationships and seek support when needed.

Set SMART Goals: Define clear, achievable goals and celebrate your progress.

Engage in Daily Practices: Incorporate journaling, meditation, and affirmations into your routine.

Participate in Activities: Join team sports, volunteer, and take up challenging hobbies.

"These strategies will help you build a solid foundation of resilience. By practicing them regularly, you'll develop the mental and emotional strength to navigate life's challenges with confidence and grace. Start today, and watch as your resilience grows, transforming your ability to face adversity and achieve your goals."

Chapter Summary

Steps to Build Resilience:

- Positive Mindset: Practice gratitude and reframe negativity.
- Emotional Regulation: Use mindfulness and deep breathing.
- Strong Connections: Build supportive relationships.
- Goal Setting: Set SMART goals and celebrate progress.
- Self-Care: Prioritize health and joy.

MINDFULNESS AND MEDITATION

Mindfulness and meditation are powerful tools for improving mental clarity, reducing stress, and enhancing overall well-being. Mindfulness involves paying full attention to the present moment and noticing your thoughts and feelings without judgment. Meditation is a practice that trains the mind to focus and achieve a state of calm and relaxation.

These practices have ancient roots but have gained significant attention in modern science. Numerous studies show that regular mindfulness and meditation can lead to profound improvements in mental and physical health. They help you develop a deeper awareness of your inner experiences and create space for thoughtful responses instead of automatic reactions.

Importance of Incorporating These Practices into Daily Life

Incorporating mindfulness and meditation into your daily routine can transform your life. Here's why:

1. **Reduces Stress and Anxiety:** Mindfulness helps you break the cycle of stress by bringing your attention to the present moment. It reduces the impact of worrying about the future or dwelling on the past.
2. **Improves Focus and Concentration:** Regular meditation enhances your ability to concentrate and stay focused on tasks. This can lead to better productivity and efficiency in both personal and professional life.
3. **Enhances Emotional Regulation:** Mindfulness allows you to become more aware of your emotions and manage them effectively. This leads to

better emotional stability and improved relationships.

4. **Promotes Physical Health:** Studies show that mindfulness and meditation can lower blood pressure, improve sleep, and boost the immune system.

Integrating these practices into your daily life doesn't require a significant time commitment. Even a few minutes each day can make a difference. By making mindfulness and meditation a habit, you can cultivate a calmer, more focused, and resilient mind.

Starting your journey with mindfulness and meditation can lead to lasting benefits. This chapter will guide you through the basics, techniques for beginners, and inspiring success stories to motivate your practice.

Benefits of Mindfulness and Meditation

Reduces Stress and Anxiety

Mindfulness calms the mind by bringing attention to the present moment. Instead of getting caught up in worries about the future or regrets about the past, mindfulness encourages you to focus on what's happening right now. This shift in focus reduces stress and anxiety.

How It Works:

Present Moment Awareness: Mindfulness helps you stay present. By paying attention to your breath, body sensations, or surroundings, you interrupt the cycle of anxious thoughts.

Non-Judgmental Observation: Observing your thoughts and feelings without judgment reduces their emotional impact. You learn to see them as temporary events, not defining aspects of yourself.

Evidence and Studies:

- **Harvard Study:** Researchers found that mindfulness meditation reduces the brain's size in the amygdala, the area associated with stress and anxiety. Participants reported feeling less stressed and more relaxed.

- **University of Massachusetts:** Studies show that an 8-week mindfulness-based stress reduction (MBSR) program significantly lowers anxiety levels in participants.

Mindfulness calms your mind by changing how you relate to your thoughts. Instead of being overwhelmed, you become an observer, which reduces stress and anxiety.

Improves Focus and Concentration

Meditation trains your brain to focus. By practicing regularly, you enhance your cognitive functions, including attention, memory, and problem-solving skills.

How It Works:

Focused Attention: Meditation involves focusing on a single point of attention, such as your breath or a mantra. This practice strengthens your ability to concentrate.

Increased Awareness: Meditation improves your awareness of distractions. When your mind wanders, you learn to gently bring it back to your focus point, enhancing your overall concentration.

Real-World Applications:

Productivity: Improved focus means better productivity. Professionals who meditate report higher efficiency and better decision-making skills.

Learning: Students who meditate show improved academic performance. Enhanced concentration and memory retention lead to better learning outcomes.

Evidence and Studies:

- **University of California, Santa Barbara:** A study found that students who practiced mindfulness meditation showed significant improvements in working memory and cognitive performance.
- **Medical College of Georgia:** Research demonstrated that just 20 minutes of meditation daily can improve attention span and cognitive function.

Meditation enhances your brain's ability to focus and concentrate, leading to better performance in everyday tasks and long-term cognitive health.

Enhances Emotional Regulation

Mindfulness and meditation improve your ability to manage emotions. By becoming more aware of your feelings, you can respond rather than react to emotional triggers.

How It Works:

Emotional Awareness: Meditation helps you recognize your emotions as they arise. This awareness allows you to understand and manage your feelings better.

Non-Reactivity: Instead of reacting impulsively, mindfulness teaches you to pause and consider your response. This leads to more thoughtful and measured reactions.

Impact on Mood and Emotional Well-Being:

1. **Reduced Reactivity:** Mindfulness reduces emotional reactivity, allowing you to handle difficult situations with greater calm and composure.
2. **Improved Mood:** Regular meditation practice is linked to higher levels of positive emotions and overall happiness.

Personal Stories of Emotional Transformation:

Sarah's Story: Sarah struggled with anger management. After starting a daily mindfulness practice, she noticed a significant change in how she handled stress. Instead of reacting angrily, she learned to pause and breathe, which helped her respond more calmly and effectively.

John's Journey: John dealt with chronic anxiety. Through meditation, he became more aware of his anxiety triggers and learned techniques to manage them. This practice transformed his approach to stressful situations, improving his overall well-being.

Evidence and Studies:

- **University of Wisconsin-Madison:** Research found that meditation practitioners showed reduced activity in the brain's areas associated with negative emotions and increased activity in areas related to positive emotions.

- **Emory University:** Studies indicate that mindfulness practices can reduce symptoms of depression and increase emotional resilience.

Mindfulness and meditation help you understand and regulate your emotions, leading to improved emotional stability and well-being.

"Mindfulness and meditation offer profound benefits, from reducing stress and anxiety to improving focus and emotional regulation. By incorporating these practices into your daily life, you can enhance your mental and emotional well-being, leading to a more balanced and fulfilling life."

Techniques and Exercises for Beginners

Mindful Breathing

Step-by-Step Guide on Practicing Mindful Breathing
Mindful breathing is the foundation of mindfulness practice. It's simple but incredibly effective at calming the mind and reducing stress.

How to Practice Mindful Breathing:

- **Find a Quiet Space:** Sit comfortably in a chair or on the floor. Close your eyes if that feels comfortable.
- **Focus on Your Breath:** Take a deep breath through your nose, feeling your lungs expand. Exhale slowly through your mouth.
- **Count Your Breaths:** Inhale for a count of four, hold for a count of four and exhale for a count of six. This helps regulate your breathing and focus your mind.
- **Notice Your Thoughts:** As you breathe, thoughts will come and go. Simply notice them without judgment and gently bring your focus back to your breath.

Tips for Integrating It into Daily Routine:

- **Morning Routine**: Start your day with five minutes of mindful breathing. It sets a calm tone for the day.
- Work Breaks:Use mindful breathing during breaks to reset and refocus.
- Evening Wind-Down: Practice before bed to relax and improve sleep quality.

Mindful breathing is a simple practice that can be done anytime, anywhere, making it easy to incorporate into your daily routine.

Body Scan Meditation

Instructions on Performing a Body Scan

Body scan meditation helps you develop a greater awareness of bodily sensations and tension.

How to Perform a Body Scan:

- **Lie Down Comfortably:** Lie on your back with your legs straight and arms at your sides. Close your eyes.
- **Focus on Your Breath:** Take a few deep breaths to center yourself.
- Start at Your Feet: Bring your attention to your toes. Notice any sensations—warmth, tingling, tension. Don't try to change anything; just observe.
- **Move Upward:** Gradually move your focus up your body—feet, legs, hips, abdomen, chest, arms, hands, neck, and head. Spend a few moments in each area, observing sensations.
- **Notice Tension and Relax:** If you find tension, breathe into that area and imagine the tension melting away as you exhale.

Benefits and When to Practice It:

Reduces Tension: Helps identify and release physical tension.
   Improves Awareness: Increases awareness of your body and its needs.
   Enhances Relaxation: Promotes deep relaxation and stress relief.
   When to Practice:

Before Bed: Helps relax the body and mind for better sleep.

After Work: Releases accumulated tension from the day.

Body scan meditation is a powerful tool for enhancing bodily awareness and promoting relaxation.

Guided Meditation

Overview of Guided Meditation and Resources

Guided meditation involves listening to a narrator who leads you through a meditation practice. It's ideal for beginners as it provides structure and guidance.

How to Practice Guided Meditation:

Choose a Quiet Space: Find a comfortable and quiet place to sit or lie down.

Select a Meditation: Use apps like Headspace, Calm, or Insight Timer. Choose a meditation that suits your needs—stress relief, focus, sleep, etc.

Follow the Guidance: Close your eyes, listen to the instructions, and follow along. The guide will lead you through breathing exercises, visualizations, or body scans.

How to Choose the Right Guided Meditation:

Identify Your Goals: Determine what you want to achieve—relaxation, focus, emotional healing.

Experiment: Try different types of guided meditations to see what resonates with you.

Use Reputable Sources: Stick to well-reviewed apps and trusted meditation teachers.

Loving-Kindness Meditation

Steps to Practice Loving-Kindness Meditation

Loving-kindness meditation, or Metta, focuses on developing compassion and sending goodwill to yourself and others.

How to Practice Loving-Kindness Meditation:

1. Find a Comfortable Position: Sit comfortably and close your eyes.
2. Focus on Your Breath: Take a few deep breaths to center yourself.
3. Start with Yourself: Silently repeat phrases like "May I be happy. May I be healthy? May I be safe? May I live with ease." Feel these intentions.
4. Extend to Others: Gradually extend these wishes to others:

- Loved Ones: "May you be happy. May you be healthy."
- Neutral People: Think of someone you don't have strong feelings about.
- Difficult People: Extend compassion to those with whom you have conflicts.
- All Beings: Finally, wish all living beings happiness and health.

How It Fosters Compassion and Reduces Negativity:

- **Increases Compassion**: Regular practice strengthens your capacity for empathy and compassion.
- **Reduces Anger and Resentment**: By extending goodwill to difficult people, you diminish feelings of anger and resentment.
- **Enhances Positive Emotions**: Boosts feelings of love, joy, and connection.

Loving-kindness meditation transforms your mindset, fostering a sense of universal compassion and reducing negative emotions.

Mindful Walking

Techniques for Practicing Mindfulness While Walking
Mindful walking combines movement with mindfulness, helping you stay present and aware during your daily walks.
How to Practice Mindful Walking:

1. **Choose Your Path:** Find a quiet place where you can walk without interruptions.
2. **Focus on Your Breath:** Begin by taking a few deep breaths to centre yourself.

3. **Pay Attention to Your Steps:** Walk slowly and deliberately. Notice the sensation of your feet touching the ground.
4. **Observe Your Surroundings:** Use all your senses. Notice the sights, sounds, smells, and sensations around you.
5. **Stay Present:** When your mind wanders, gently bring your attention back to your walking and breathing.

Benefits and Examples of Mindful Walking Routines:

- **Reduces Stress:** Combines the benefits of physical activity and mindfulness, lowering stress levels.
- **Improves Mood:** Being outdoors and moving mindfully boosts your mood and energy.
- **Enhances Focus:** Helps clear your mind and improve concentration.

Examples of Routines:

Morning Walks: Start your day with a 10-15 minute mindful walk to set a positive tone.

Break Time: Use your lunch break for a quick mindful walk to refresh and recharge.

Evening Strolls: Wind down with a mindful walk in the evening to relax and reflect on your day.

Mindful walking is an accessible and effective way to incorporate mindfulness into your daily life while enjoying the benefits of physical activity.

"These techniques provide practical, easy-to-follow steps for integrating mindfulness and meditation into your routine. By practicing mindful breathing, body scan meditation, guided meditation, loving-kindness meditation, and mindful walking, you can enhance your mental and emotional well-being. Start small, stay consistent, and watch as these practices transform your life."

Success Stories of Individuals Who Have Adopted Mindfulness Practices

Story 1: Reducing Work-Related Stress

Background and Challenges Faced

Jane, a marketing executive, constantly dealt with high-pressure deadlines and a demanding workload. The stress started affecting her sleep, mood, and overall well-being. She often felt overwhelmed and struggled to maintain her performance at work.

How Mindfulness Helped Manage Stress

Jane decided to try mindfulness to manage her stress better. She started with simple practices like mindful breathing and short guided meditations during her lunch breaks. She also incorporated body scan meditations in the evenings to unwind and relax.

Outcome and Current Practices

Within a few weeks, Jane noticed significant improvements. She felt more focused and less reactive to work stress. Her sleep quality improved, and she began to enjoy her work again. Today, Jane practices mindfulness daily, starting her morning with a 10-minute meditation and using mindful breathing techniques during stressful moments at work. Her stress levels are much lower, and she feels more balanced and in control.

Story 2: Overcoming Anxiety

Personal Struggles with Anxiety

Tom, a college student, battled severe anxiety that affected his academic performance and social life. He often experienced panic attacks and found it hard to concentrate on his studies. The constant worry about his grades and future made his anxiety worse.

Mindfulness Techniques Used

Tom's therapist recommended mindfulness practices to help manage his anxiety. He began with mindful breathing exercises to calm his mind during anxious moments. Tom also practiced guided meditations focused on relaxation and anxiety relief. Additionally, he started journaling to track his thoughts and feelings.

Transformation and Improvement

Over time, Tom's anxiety significantly decreased. The mindful breathing exercises helped him manage panic attacks, and the guided meditations provided a sense of calm and clarity. Journaling allowed him to identify and challenge negative thought patterns. Now, Tom practices mindfulness daily, incorporating it into his study routine and social interactions. His academic performance improved, and he feels more confident and less anxious.

Story 3: Enhancing Focus and Productivity

Initial Productivity Issues

Laura, a project manager, struggled with maintaining focus and productivity. She was easily distracted and often found herself procrastinating. Her lack of focus led to missed deadlines and increased stress.

Mindfulness Practices Adopted

To improve her focus, Laura adopted mindfulness practices. She started with short daily meditations to enhance her concentration. Laura also practiced mindful walking during her breaks to clear her mind and refocus. Additionally, she used mindful breathing techniques before starting any major task to set a calm and focused mindset.

Results and Sustained Benefits

Laura experienced a significant boost in her productivity. The regular meditation practice improved her attention span and reduced distractions. Mindful walking and breathing helped her stay calm and focused throughout the day. As a result, she met her deadlines more consistently and with less stress. Laura continues to practice mindfulness daily, crediting it with her improved work performance and overall well-being.

Story 4: Emotional Healing

Emotional Challenges and Impact on Life

Sarah, a nurse, faced emotional burnout from her demanding job. The constant exposure to stress and suffering took a toll on her mental health. She felt emotionally drained, and this impacted her personal life and relationships.

Role of Meditation in Emotional Healing

Sarah turned to meditation for emotional healing. She started with loving-kindness meditation, focusing on fostering compassion for herself and others. Sarah also practiced guided meditations aimed at emotional release and healing. She incorporated these practices into her daily routine, dedicating time each morning and evening to meditate.

Long-Term Effects and Continued Practice

The impact of meditation on Sarah's emotional health was profound. She felt more compassionate and patient, both at work and in her personal life. The loving-kindness meditation helped her reconnect with her sense of empathy and purpose. Sarah's relationships improved, and she felt more balanced and emotionally resilient. She continues to practice meditation daily, finding it an essential tool for maintaining her emotional well-being and professional satisfaction.

"These success stories highlight the transformative power of mindfulness and meditation. From reducing work-related stress and overcoming anxiety to enhancing focus and emotional healing, these practices offer practical solutions for managing life's challenges. By incorporating mindfulness into daily routines, individuals can achieve lasting improvements in their mental and emotional well-being."

Practical Tips for Sustaining Mindfulness Practices

How to Build a Consistent Mindfulness Routine

Building a consistent mindfulness routine starts with simplicity and commitment. Start small to make it manageable and gradually build up. Begin with just five minutes each day, either in the morning or before bed. Set a specific time and place for your practice to create a habit. Use reminders, such as phone alarms or sticky notes, to keep you on track.

Steps to Build Consistency:

- **Start Small:** Begin with short, daily sessions.
- **Set a Routine:** Choose a specific time and place.
- **Use Reminders:** Set phone alarms or place notes where you'll see them.

- **Stay Accountable**: Share your goals with a friend or join a mindfulness group.

Overcoming Common Challenges and Staying Motivated

Staying motivated can be challenging, especially when starting. It's normal to encounter obstacles, such as feeling too busy or struggling with distractions. Acknowledge these challenges and remind yourself of the benefits.

Tips to Overcome Challenges:

- **Forgive Yourself:** If you miss a session, don't be hard on yourself. Simply start again.
- **Mix It Up:** Try different types of mindfulness practices to keep it interesting.
- **Track Your Progress:** Use a journal to note improvements and reflect on your journey.
- **Celebrate Small Wins:** Acknowledge your consistency and the positive changes you notice.

By starting small, setting a routine, and addressing challenges head-on, you can build and sustain a rewarding mindfulness practice.

Chapter Summary:

- **Mindful Breathing**: Practice focusing on your breath to anchor yourself in the present moment and reduce stress.
- **Body Scan Meditation**: Increase bodily awareness by focusing on sensations from head to toe, promoting relaxation and stress relief.
- **Guided Meditation**: Use apps and resources for structured meditation sessions to help beginners get started.
- **Loving-Kindness Meditation:** Foster compassion and reduce negativity by sending goodwill to yourself and others.

- **Mindful Walking:** Practice mindfulness while walking by focusing on your movements and surroundings, enhancing awareness and relaxation.

Steps to Integrate Mindfulness:

- **Start Small:** Begin with short, manageable sessions.
- **Be Consistent:** Practice at the same time each day.
- **Stay Flexible:** Adjust your practice to fit your lifestyle.

CHAPTER EIGHT

TIME MANAGEMENT AND PRIORITIZATION

Time management and prioritization are essential skills for navigating the demands of modern life. Effective time management allows you to allocate your time efficiently, ensuring that important tasks get done without overwhelming yourself. Prioritization helps you determine which tasks are most critical and deserve your immediate attention.

These skills are not just about being busy; they are about being productive. By mastering time management and prioritization, you can make the most of your day, achieve your goals, and maintain a healthy work-life balance.

Importance of Effective Time Management

Reduces Stress and Overwhelm

Effective time management significantly reduces stress and feelings of overwhelm. When you manage your time well, you feel more in control of your tasks and responsibilities. Instead of reacting to the demands of the day, you can proactively plan your activities.

How It Lowers Stress Levels:

Clear Priorities: By setting clear priorities, you know exactly what needs to be done and when. This clarity reduces the mental load of constantly deciding what to tackle next.

Structured Plan: A structured plan helps you avoid last-minute rushes. Knowing you have allocated time for each task means you can approach your day with confidence and calm.

Realistic Goals: Effective time management involves setting realistic goals. By not overcommitting, you avoid the stress of trying to do too much in too little time.

Examples of Common Stressors Related to Poor Time Management:

Missed Deadlines: Constantly missing deadlines create anxiety and a sense of failure.

Overcommitment: Taking on too many tasks leads to burnout and frustration.

Procrastination: Delaying important tasks increases stress as deadlines loom closer.

By managing your time effectively, you can mitigate these stressors and create a more balanced and peaceful life.

Increases Productivity

Prioritizing tasks and managing your time efficiently leads to higher productivity. When you focus on the most important tasks first, you ensure that your energy and resources are used effectively.

How Prioritizing Tasks Leads to Higher Productivity:

Focus on High-Impact Activities: By identifying and prioritizing high-impact tasks, you can make significant progress in key areas. This focus ensures that your efforts yield the best results.

Reduced Multitasking: Multitasking can dilute your focus and efficiency. Prioritizing allows you to concentrate on one task at a time, increasing the quality and speed of your work.

Better Use of Energy: Tackling important tasks when your energy levels are highest leads to better performance and less fatigue.

Impact on Both Personal and Professional Life:

Professional Life: Higher productivity at work can lead to better performance reviews, promotions, and job satisfaction. By managing your time well, you can meet deadlines, produce high-quality work, and achieve your career goals.

Personal Life: Effective time management frees up time for personal interests and relationships. By being more productive, you can enjoy leisure activities, pursue hobbies, and spend quality time with loved ones.

Prioritizing tasks and managing your time efficiently not only boosts your productivity but also enhances your overall quality of life.

Enhances Work-Life Balance

Balancing work demands with personal life is essential for long-term happiness and well-being. Effective time management plays a crucial role in achieving this balance.

Strategies for Balancing Work Demands with Personal Life:

Set Boundaries: Establish clear boundaries between work and personal time. This might mean not checking work emails after a certain hour or dedicating weekends to family and relaxation.

Schedule Personal Time: Just as you schedule work tasks, schedule personal activities. Make time for exercise, hobbies, and socializing. Treat these commitments as non-negotiable.

Prioritize Self-Care: Self-care is critical for maintaining energy and motivation. Allocate time for activities that recharge you, whether it's reading, walking, or simply relaxing.

The Role of Time Management in Achieving a Healthy Work-Life Balance:

Structured Routine: A well-structured routine ensures that you allocate time for both work and personal life. This structure prevents work from encroaching on personal time and vice versa.

Flexibility: While structure is important, flexibility is also key. Effective time management allows for adjustments when unexpected events arise, ensuring that one area of life doesn't suffer due to unforeseen demands in another.

Efficiency: Managing your time efficiently means you can complete work tasks within the designated time, leaving ample room for personal activities. This efficiency reduces the need for overtime and helps prevent burnout.

By implementing these strategies and managing your time effectively, you can create a healthy balance between work and personal life. This balance leads to greater satisfaction, improved relationships, and better overall health.

"Mastering time management is crucial for reducing stress, increasing productivity, and achieving a balanced life. By setting clear priorities, focusing on high-impact tasks, and scheduling time for personal activities, you can take control of your time and enhance both your professional and personal well-being."

Practical Tips and Tools for Prioritization

Eisenhower Matrix

Explanation of the Eisenhower Matrix

The Eisenhower Matrix, also known as the Urgent-Important Matrix, is a powerful tool for prioritizing tasks. It helps you categorize tasks based on their urgency and importance, allowing you to focus on what truly matters.

The matrix is divided into four quadrants:

Urgent and Important (Quadrant I): Tasks that need immediate attention and have significant consequences. These are your top priorities.

Not Urgent but Important (Quadrant II): Tasks that are important but not time-sensitive. These activities help you achieve long-term goals and should be scheduled.

Urgent but Not Important (Quadrant III): Tasks that require immediate attention but do not contribute significantly to your long-term goals. These can often be delegated.

Not Urgent and Not Important (Quadrant IV): Tasks that are neither urgent nor important. These activities are distractions and should be minimized or eliminated.

How to Categorize Tasks by Urgency and Importance

List Your Tasks: Write down all the tasks you need to complete.

Assess Urgency: Determine which tasks need to be done immediately and which can wait.

Evaluate Importance: Identify tasks that align with your long-term goals and values.

Place Tasks in Quadrants: Categorize each task into one of the four quadrants.

Practical Examples of Using the Matrix

Quadrant I (Urgent and Important): A project deadline tomorrow, an urgent client meeting.

Quadrant II (Not Urgent but Important): Long-term strategic planning, personal development activities.

Quadrant III (Urgent but Not Important): Answering non-critical emails, and attending unproductive meetings.

Quadrant IV (Not Urgent and Not Important): Browsing social media, unnecessary chores.

Using the Eisenhower Matrix helps you focus on what truly matters, reduces stress, and increases productivity by ensuring you spend your time on tasks that have the most significant impact.

ABC Method

Overview of the ABC Method for Task Prioritization

The ABC Method is a simple and effective way to prioritize tasks based on their importance. It categorizes tasks into three groups:

A Tasks (High Priority): Tasks that are crucial and must be done immediately.

B Tasks (Medium Priority): Important tasks that are not as urgent as A tasks.

C Tasks (Low Priority): Tasks that are nice to do but have little impact on your goals.

Steps to Implement the ABC Method in Daily Planning

List Your Tasks: Write down all the tasks you need to complete.

Assign Priorities: Label each task as A, B, or C based on its importance and urgency.

Tackle A Tasks First: Start your day by completing A tasks. These are your top priorities and should be done first.

Move to B Tasks: Once A tasks are completed, focus on B tasks. These are important but less urgent.

Handle C Tasks: If time permits, work on C tasks. These tasks are not critical and can often be postponed or delegated.

Real-Life Applications and Benefits

Workplace: Use the ABC Method to prioritize work tasks. Focus on high-impact projects (A tasks), then move to less critical work (B tasks), and finally address minor tasks (C tasks).

Personal Life: Apply the ABC Method to personal tasks, such as fitness goals (A tasks), home maintenance (B tasks), and hobbies (C tasks).

Benefits:

Clear Prioritization: This helps you focus on what matters most.

Improved Productivity: Ensures that high-priority tasks are completed first.

Reduced Stress: Organizes your day and prevents overwhelm by breaking down tasks into manageable categories.

The ABC Method simplifies task management, making it easier to prioritize and complete tasks efficiently.

Time Blocking

Introduction to Time Blocking Technique

Time blocking is a technique where you allocate specific time slots to different tasks or activities throughout your day. This method helps you stay focused and ensures that each task gets dedicated attention.

How to Allocate Specific Time Slots for Different Tasks

List Your Tasks: Write down all the tasks you need to complete for the day.

Estimate Time Required: Determine how long each task will take.

Create a Schedule: Block out specific times for each task on your calendar. Include breaks and buffer time.

Stick to the Schedule: Follow your time blocks as closely as possible to maintain focus and productivity.

Tips for Effective Time Blocking

Start with High-Priority Tasks: Allocate time for your most important tasks first, usually at the beginning of the day when your energy is highest.

Group Similar Tasks: Block similar tasks together to minimize context switching and increase efficiency.

Include Breaks: Schedule regular breaks to rest and recharge. This helps maintain productivity throughout the day.

Be Realistic: Ensure that your time blocks are realistic and achievable. Avoid over-scheduling and allow flexibility for unexpected tasks.

Example of a Time-Blocked Day:

8:00 AM - 9:00 AM: Morning routine and planning.

9:00 AM - 11:00 AM: High-priority project work.

11:00 AM - 11:30 AM: Break.

11:30 AM - 1:00 PM: Emails and administrative tasks.

1:00 PM - 2:00 PM: Lunch break.

2:00 PM - 3:30 PM: Client meetings.

3:30 PM - 4:00 PM: Break.

4:00 PM - 5:30 PM: Secondary tasks and planning for the next day.

Time blocking helps you manage your day efficiently, ensuring that each task receives focused attention and reducing the likelihood of distractions.

Pomodoro Technique

Explanation of the Pomodoro Technique

The Pomodoro Technique is a time management method developed by Francesco Cirillo in the late 1980s. It uses a timer to break work into intervals, traditionally 25 minutes in length, separated by short breaks.

How to Use Timed Work Sessions to Improve Focus

Choose a Task: Select a task you want to work on.

Set a Timer: Set a timer for 25 minutes (one Pomodoro).
Work on the Task: Focus solely on the task until the timer rings.
Take a Short Break: Take a 5-minute break to rest.
Repeat: After four Pomodoros, take a longer break (15-30 minutes).

Benefits of the Pomodoro Technique for Productivity

Enhanced Focus: The fixed work intervals help you maintain focus and avoid distractions.

Increased Productivity: Frequent breaks prevent burnout and keep you fresh, allowing you to work more efficiently.

Better Time Awareness: The Pomodoro Technique helps you understand how long tasks take, improving your time estimation skills.

Example of a Pomodoro Schedule:

8:00 AM - 8:25 AM: Work on writing a report (Pomodoro 1).
8:25 AM - 8:30 AM: Break.
8:30 AM - 8:55 AM: Continue writing the report (Pomodoro 2).
8:55 AM - 9:00 AM: Break.
9:00 AM - 9:25 AM: Review and edit the report (Pomodoro 3).
9:25 AM - 9:30 AM: Break.
9:30 AM - 9:55 AM: Start new project planning (Pomodoro 4).
9:55 AM - 10:25 AM: Longer break.
The Pomodoro Technique helps break work into manageable intervals, boosting focus and productivity through structured work and rest periods.

Digital Tools and Apps

Overview of Popular Time Management Apps
Digital tools and apps can significantly enhance your time management and prioritization efforts. Here are a few popular options:
Trello: A project management tool that uses boards, lists, and cards to help you organize tasks and collaborate with others.
Asana: A comprehensive task and project management app that allows you to track work, set deadlines, and manage team projects.
Todoist: A task management app that helps you create and organize tasks, set due dates, and track your progress.

Notion: An all-in-one workspace that combines note-taking, task management, and collaboration tools.

How Digital Tools Can Assist in Prioritization and Task Management

Task Organization: Digital tools help you organize tasks by projects, deadlines, and priority levels.

Reminders and Notifications: Set reminders to ensure you don't miss important deadlines.

Collaboration: Easily share tasks and projects with team members, facilitating better collaboration and communication.

Progress Tracking: Track your progress and adjust your plans as needed.

"By leveraging digital tools, you can streamline your task management, improve prioritization, and boost productivity, making it easier to stay on top of your responsibilities."

Case Studies of Improved Productivity and Reduced Pressure

Case Study 1: Professional Success

Background

Lisa, a marketing manager at a mid-sized company, struggled with managing her workload. Constantly overwhelmed by deadlines and meetings, she found it difficult to focus on high-priority tasks. Her productivity suffered, and work pressure affected her health and personal life.

Techniques Used

Lisa implemented several time management strategies to regain control. She started using the Eisenhower Matrix to prioritize her tasks by urgency and importance. She also adopted time blocking to allocate specific periods for focused work, meetings, and breaks.

Outcome

Within a few weeks, Lisa's productivity improved significantly. By focusing on high-priority tasks first and scheduling her day effectively, she was able to meet deadlines with ease. The reduced work pressure allowed her to maintain a healthier work-life balance, leading to better overall well-being and job satisfaction.

"Source: Harvard Business Review on Time Management"

Case Study 2: Academic Achievement

Background

Mark, a college student majoring in engineering, faced significant academic stress. Juggling multiple courses and assignments, he found it challenging to manage his time effectively. His grades were suffering, and he experienced constant anxiety about his academic performance.

Techniques Used

Mark decided to use the ABC Method for task prioritization. He categorized his assignments and study tasks into A (high priority), B (medium priority), and C (low priority). Additionally, he created a study schedule using time blocking to ensure dedicated study periods for each subject.

Outcome

By prioritizing his tasks and following a structured study schedule, Mark saw a noticeable improvement in his grades. The methodical approach helped him manage his workload more efficiently, reducing his anxiety. Mark's confidence grew as he consistently met his academic goals, and his overall stress levels decreased.

"Source: University of Cambridge Study Tips"

Case Study 3: Work-Life Balance

Background

Sarah, a software developer, struggled to balance her demanding job with her personal life. Late nights at the office and weekend work left her with little time for family, friends, or self-care. Her stress levels were high, and her personal relationships were strained.

Techniques Used

Sarah adopted time blocking and set firm boundaries between work and personal time. She scheduled her work tasks during office hours and blocked out evenings and weekends for personal activities. She also used the Pomodoro Technique to maintain focus and productivity during her work hours.

Outcome

By creating a clear separation between work and personal time, Sarah achieved a healthier work-life balance. Her productivity at work improved, as did her personal happiness. Regular breaks and focused work periods prevented burnout, and she enjoyed more quality time with her family and friends.

"Source: Forbes on Work-Life Balance"

Case Study 4: Entrepreneurial Efficiency

Background

David, an entrepreneur running a tech startup, struggled with managing multiple responsibilities. From product development to marketing and sales, he found it challenging to prioritize tasks effectively. The constant juggling led to inefficiencies and increased stress.

Techniques Used

David turned to digital tools like Trello and Asana to manage his tasks. He used these platforms to prioritize tasks, set deadlines, and delegate responsibilities. Additionally, he implemented the Eisenhower Matrix to focus on high-impact activities and reduce time spent on less critical tasks.

Outcome

Using digital tools and prioritization methods, David increased his business efficiency. He streamlined his workflow, delegated tasks effectively, and focused on strategic activities. The reduced pressure and improved organization allowed David to drive his startup forward with greater clarity and purpose, leading to personal satisfaction and business growth.

"Source: Entrepreneur on Using Digital Tools for Efficiency"

These case studies highlight the transformative impact of effective time management and prioritization. From professional success and academic achievement to work-life balance and entrepreneurial efficiency, these examples demonstrate how practical strategies can lead to significant improvements in productivity and reduced pressure.

Practical Exercises and Actionable Steps

Daily Time Audit

How to Conduct a Time Audit to Identify Time-Wasting Activities

A daily time audit helps you understand how you spend your time and identify areas for improvement. Start by tracking all your activities throughout the day. Use a simple spreadsheet or a time-tracking app to log each task, along with the time spent on it.

Steps to Streamline Daily Tasks and Improve Efficiency

Track Your Activities: For one week, note down every activity you engage in, including work tasks, meetings, breaks, and leisure activities. Be honest and detailed.

Analyze the Data: At the end of the week, review your log. Identify patterns, such as time spent on low-priority tasks, frequent interruptions, or prolonged breaks.

Identify Time Wasters: Highlight activities that don't contribute to your goals or productivity. Common time wasters include excessive social media use, unproductive meetings, and multitasking.

Set Priorities: Categorize your tasks based on their importance and urgency using the Eisenhower Matrix or ABC Method.

Create an Action Plan: Develop strategies to minimize or eliminate time-wasting activities. For example, limit social media use to specific times, streamline meetings with clear agendas, and focus on one task at a time.

By conducting a time audit, you gain insight into how you spend your day and can make targeted changes to improve efficiency and productivity.

Goal Setting and Planning

Setting SMART Goals and Breaking Them Down into Manageable Tasks

SMART goals are Specific, Measurable, Achievable, Relevant, and Time-bound. Setting SMART goals helps you create clear and actionable objectives.

Steps to Set and Achieve SMART Goals:

Define Your Goals: Write down what you want to achieve, ensuring each goal is specific and clear.

Make Them Measurable: Identify metrics to track your progress. For example, if your goal is to improve fitness, track workout frequency and duration.

Ensure They Are Achievable: Set realistic goals that challenge you but are within your reach.

Keep Them Relevant: Align your goals with your long-term objectives and values.

Set a Time Frame: Establish deadlines to create a sense of urgency and motivation.

Tips for Effective Daily and Weekly Planning

Break Down Goals: Divide each goal into smaller, manageable tasks. For example, if your goal is to write a book, break it down into tasks like outlining chapters, writing drafts, and editing.

Prioritize Tasks: Use the ABC Method or Eisenhower Matrix to prioritize your tasks.

Create a Schedule: Plan your week in advance, allocating specific time slots for each task. Use time blocking to stay focused.

Review and Adjust: At the end of each day and week, review your progress and adjust your plan as needed.

By setting SMART goals and planning effectively, you can stay organized, motivated, and on track to achieve your objectives.

Developing a Routine

Creating a Consistent Daily Routine to Maximize Productivity

A consistent daily routine helps you manage your time efficiently and build productive habits. Start by structuring your day around high-priority tasks and regular activities.

Steps to Develop an Effective Daily Routine:

Identify Key Activities: List the essential tasks and activities you need to include in your routine, such as work, exercise, meals, and relaxation.

Set a Schedule: Assign specific times for each activity. For example, schedule your most important work tasks during your peak productivity hours.

Include Breaks: Incorporate regular breaks to rest and recharge. Use techniques like the Pomodoro Technique to structure work and break periods.

Be Consistent: Stick to your routine as closely as possible. Consistency builds habits and reduces decision fatigue.

Incorporating Breaks and Leisure Activities for Better Time Management

Scheduled Breaks: Plan short breaks throughout your workday to maintain focus and prevent burnout. For example, take a 5-minute break every 25 minutes using the Pomodoro Technique.

Leisure Activities: Dedicate time each day to activities you enjoy, such as hobbies, exercise, or socializing. This helps balance work and personal life.

Evening Routine: Create a wind-down routine in the evening to relax and prepare for the next day. This might include activities like reading, meditation, or light exercise.

Flexibility: Allow some flexibility in your routine to accommodate unexpected events or changes. Adjust your schedule as needed while maintaining your overall structure.

Developing a consistent daily routine with regular breaks and leisure activities enhances your productivity and well-being, helping you achieve a balanced and fulfilling life.

Chapter Summary

- Eisenhower Matrix: Prioritize tasks by urgency and importance using four quadrants.
- ABC Method: Categorize tasks into A (high priority), B (medium priority), and C (low priority) to focus on what matters most.
- Time Blocking: Allocate specific time slots for different tasks to maintain focus and productivity.
- Pomodoro Technique: Use 25-minute work intervals followed by short breaks to improve concentration and efficiency.
- Digital Tools and Apps: Utilize tools like Trello, Asana, and Todoist to organize tasks, set deadlines, and track progress.
- Practical Exercises: Conduct a daily time audit, set SMART goals, and develop a consistent routine with breaks and leisure activities.

CHAPTER NINE

CREATING A SUPPORT SYSTEM

Importance of a Strong Support System

A strong support system is one of the most valuable assets you can have. It's the foundation that helps you navigate life's challenges with resilience and confidence. Whether you're facing personal struggles, professional hurdles, or simply the ups and downs of everyday life, having a network of supportive relationships can make all the difference.

Supportive relationships provide emotional comfort, practical assistance, and a sense of belonging. They offer different perspectives and advice, helping you see situations more clearly and make better decisions. A strong support system acts as a buffer against stress, reducing its impact on your mental and physical health.

How Supportive Relationships Enhance Resilience and Well-Being

Resilience is your ability to bounce back from adversity, and well-being is your overall sense of health and happiness. Supportive relationships play a crucial role in both. Here's how:

- Emotional Support: Friends, family, and colleagues can provide a listening ear and compassionate advice during tough times. This emotional support helps you process your feelings and reduces the burden of stress.

- Practical Help: Whether it's offering a hand with daily tasks or providing resources and information, supportive relationships offer practical help that makes life's challenges more manageable.
- Motivation and Encouragement: A strong support system encourages you to pursue your goals and dreams. The positive reinforcement from those who believe in you boosts your confidence and motivation.
- Sense of Belonging: Being part of a community or network gives you a sense of belonging and connectedness. This social connection is vital for mental health and well-being.

In this chapter, we'll explore how to build and maintain supportive relationships, and we'll hear stories of individuals who have thrived with the help of strong support systems. By the end, you'll understand the profound impact these relationships can have on your resilience and well-being.

Building Supportive Relationships

Identifying Key Relationships

Building a strong support system starts with identifying the key relationships in your life. These relationships can be categorized into four main types: family, friends, colleagues, and mentors. Each plays a unique role in providing support and enhancing your well-being.

Family

Family is often the cornerstone of your support system. These are the people who know you best and have a deep, unconditional bond with you. Family members can offer emotional support, practical help, and a sense of belonging that is hard to find elsewhere. They provide a stable foundation and are typically there for you in times of crisis.

Friends

Friends add another layer of support, bringing joy, companionship, and a different perspective to your life. They can offer advice, share experiences, and provide a listening ear. Friendships often come with a mutual understanding and shared interests, making them a vital part of your emotional support network.

Colleagues

Colleagues play a significant role in your professional support system. These relationships can provide career guidance, collaboration opportunities, and a sense of camaraderie at work. Supportive colleagues can help you navigate workplace challenges and celebrate professional successes.

Mentors

Mentors are invaluable for personal and professional growth. They offer wisdom, guidance, and advice based on their own experiences. A mentor can help you see the bigger picture, set goals, and stay motivated. Their support is instrumental in achieving long-term success.

By recognizing and nurturing these key relationships, you can build a robust support system that helps you navigate life's challenges and enhances your overall well-being.

Cultivating Strong Connections

Building strong connections requires effort, trust, and mutual respect. Here are some tips to help you cultivate these essential elements in your relationships.

Building Trust

Trust is the foundation of any strong relationship. To build trust, be consistent and reliable. Keep your promises and show that you can be depended upon. Honesty is crucial—be open and transparent in your communications. Trust also involves showing vulnerability and allowing others to see your authentic self.

Mutual Respect

Mutual respect involves valuing each other's opinions, feelings, and boundaries. Show appreciation and gratitude for the support you receive, and be mindful of the other person's needs and perspectives. Respect their time and efforts, and recognize that healthy relationships are built on equality and reciprocity.

Regular Communication

Regular communication is key to maintaining strong connections. Make an effort to stay in touch, whether it's through calls, texts, or face-to-face meetings. Share your experiences, listen actively, and show genuine interest in the other person's life. Consistent communication helps strengthen the bond and keeps the relationship vibrant.

Quality Time

Spending quality time together is essential for deepening connections. Engage in activities you both enjoy and create shared experiences. Whether it's having dinner together, going for a walk, or simply chatting over coffee, these moments foster closeness and understanding.

By focusing on trust, mutual respect, regular communication, and quality time, you can cultivate strong, supportive relationships that enrich your life.

Balancing Give and Take

Healthy relationships are built on a balance of giving and receiving. Ensuring reciprocity in your relationship not only strengthens the bond but also makes both parties feel valued and supported.

Ensuring Reciprocity

Reciprocity means that both parties contribute to and benefit from the relationship. It's important to be mindful of the balance between giving and taking. If you find yourself always on the giving end, it might lead to burnout or resentment. Conversely, if you're always taking, it might strain the relationship and lead to feelings of guilt or dependency.

How to Support Others

Supporting others involves being there for them emotionally and practically. Listen actively when they share their concerns, offer help when needed, and provide encouragement. Small gestures, like checking in with a text or helping with a task, show that you care. Be present and attentive, and make sure to respect their boundaries.

Seeking Support

Don't hesitate to seek support when you need it. Being open about your struggles and asking for help fosters a deeper connection. It shows that you trust the other person and value their support. Remember, it's okay to lean on others—relationships are a two-way street, and seeking help when needed strengthens the bond.

Maintaining Balance

To maintain a healthy balance, regularly assess the dynamics of your relationships. Are you giving and receiving equally? If not, adjust your approach to ensure that both parties feel valued and supported. Communicate openly about your needs and be receptive to the needs of others.

"Balancing give and take in your relationships ensures that both parties feel appreciated and supported, creating a strong and resilient support system."

Maintaining Supportive Relationships

Consistency and Reliability

Importance of Being Dependable and Consistent in Your Relationships

Consistency and reliability are the cornerstones of any strong relationship. Being dependable means that others can count on you when they need support, advice, or a listening ear. Consistency builds trust, showing that you are a stable and reliable presence in their lives. When you are consistent in your actions and words, you strengthen the foundation of your relationships, making them more resilient to challenges.

Strategies for Staying Connected Over Time

- **Regular Check-Ins:** Make it a habit to check in with your friends, family, and colleagues regularly. Whether it's a quick text, a phone call, or a coffee meetup, consistent communication keeps the relationship alive and healthy.
- **Schedule Quality Time:** Allocate specific times in your calendar for spending time with your loved ones. Treat these appointments with the same importance as work meetings. This ensures that your relationships get the attention they deserve.
- **Follow Through on Promises:** If you commit to doing something, make sure you follow through. This builds trust and shows that you value the relationship. Reliability is demonstrated through actions, not just words.
- **Be Present:** When you are with someone, be fully present. Put away distractions like your phone and focus on the conversation. Active listening and genuine engagement show that you value their time and presence.

By being dependable and consistent, you reinforce the trust and stability in your relationships, ensuring they remain strong and supportive over time.

Handling Conflicts

Effective Communication and Conflict Resolution Techniques
Conflict is a natural part of any relationship. How you handle it can either strengthen or weaken the bond. Effective communication is key to resolving conflicts in a healthy way.

Active Listening: Truly listen to the other person's perspective without interrupting. Acknowledge their feelings and show empathy. Sometimes, just feeling heard can diffuse tension.

Stay Calm and Respectful: Approach conflicts with a calm demeanour. Avoid raising your voice or using accusatory language. Respect the other person's feelings and viewpoints, even if you disagree.

Focus on Solutions: Instead of dwelling on the problem, work together to find a solution. This shifts the focus from blame to collaboration, fostering a more positive interaction.

Use "I" Statements: Frame your concerns using "I" statements to express how you feel without blaming the other person. For example, say "I feel upset when..." instead of "You always...".

Maintaining Healthy Boundaries While Resolving Issues

Healthy boundaries are crucial in any relationship, especially during conflicts. Boundaries help protect your well-being and ensure that the relationship remains respectful.

Communicate Your Boundaries: Clearly express your boundaries and why they are important to you. Respect the other person's boundaries as well.

Take Breaks if Needed: If a conflict becomes too heated, it's okay to take a break and revisit the conversation later. This prevents saying things in the heat of the moment that you might regret.

Agree to Disagree: Sometimes, it's okay to have different opinions. Agreeing to disagree while respecting each other's perspectives can maintain harmony.

By handling conflicts with effective communication and maintaining healthy boundaries, you can resolve issues in a way that strengthens your relationships.

Nurturing Growth

Encouraging Personal and Mutual Growth in Relationships
A strong relationship is one where both parties support each other's growth. Encouraging personal and mutual development keeps the relationship dynamic and fulfilling.

Celebrate Achievements: Acknowledge and celebrate each other's successes, no matter how small. This creates a positive environment where both parties feel valued and motivated.

Encourage Learning: Support each other in pursuing new skills, hobbies, or knowledge. This could be as simple as taking a class together or sharing interesting books and articles.

Set Goals Together: Discuss and set mutual goals, whether personal, professional, or relationship-oriented. Working towards common objectives strengthens the bond and gives you a shared purpose.

Offer Constructive Feedback: Provide honest, constructive feedback that helps the other person grow. Do this with kindness and respect, focusing on how they can improve rather than criticizing.

Celebrating Successes and Supporting Through Challenges

Celebrating successes and providing support during tough times are vital aspects of a nurturing relationship.

Recognize Milestones: Celebrate important milestones, such as anniversaries, promotions, or personal achievements. This reinforces the importance of the relationship and shows that you care.

Be a Source of Strength: During challenging times, be a source of support and encouragement. Offer practical help, a listening ear, or simply your presence to show you care.

Stay Positive: Maintain a positive attitude and offer hope and optimism. This can be incredibly uplifting for someone going through a difficult period.

Show Appreciation: Regularly express your gratitude and appreciation for the other person. Simple gestures like a thank-you note or a kind word can go a long way in nurturing the relationship.

By encouraging growth, celebrating successes, and providing unwavering support, you nurture and strengthen your relationships, ensuring they remain a positive and enriching part of your life.

"Maintaining supportive relationships requires consistency, effective conflict resolution, and mutual growth. By being dependable, handling conflicts with care, and nurturing each other's growth, you can build and sustain strong, resilient relationships that enhance your well-being and resilience."

Stories of Individuals with Strong Support Systems

Story 1: Family Support

Background

John faced significant personal challenges after losing his job. The stress of unemployment, coupled with the pressure to support his family, took a toll on his mental health. Feeling overwhelmed and isolated, John struggled to see a way forward.

Outcome

During this tough period, John's family became his rock. His wife offered unwavering emotional support, listening to his fears and helping him stay positive. His parents pitched in with financial assistance, easing the immediate burden. His siblings frequently checked in, providing encouragement and practical advice. With his family's help, John found the strength to start job hunting again. Their belief in him bolstered his resilience and well-being, allowing him to land a new job within a few months. The experience brought them closer and reinforced the power of a strong family support system.

Story 2: Friendships and Peer Support

Background

Emily went through a difficult period after moving to a new city for her job. She felt lonely and disconnected, struggling to adapt to her new environment and cope with work-related stress. The lack of familiar faces and support made her feel anxious and isolated.

Outcome

Emily decided to reach out to her peers at work and in her neighbourhood. She joined a local book club and started attending social events organized by her colleagues. Gradually, she built a network of friends who shared similar interests and experiences. These friendships provided her with emotional support and practical advice. When she felt overwhelmed, her friends were there to listen and offer guidance. Their support significantly improved her mental health and confidence. With their encouragement, Emily began to thrive in her new environment, finding joy and stability in her daily life.

Story 3: Professional and Mentorship Support

Background

David, an aspiring entrepreneur, struggled to grow his startup. Despite having a great product, he lacked business experience and felt lost navigating the complexities of running a company. The stress of managing his startup alone began to weigh heavily on him.

Outcome

David sought the guidance of a mentor, an experienced business leader in his industry. His mentor provided valuable insights into business strategy, marketing, and operations. More importantly, the mentor offered emotional support, helping David stay motivated and focused. Regular meetings and feedback sessions with his mentor kept David on track, boosting his confidence and decision-making skills. With this support, David successfully scaled his startup, achieving significant milestones and personal growth. The mentor's guidance was instrumental in his journey, demonstrating the profound impact of professional and mentorship support on career development and personal fulfilment.

Story 4: Community and Social Networks

Background

Sara, a single mother, faced numerous challenges balancing work, parenting, and personal time. The stress of managing everything on her own left her exhausted and isolated. She longed for a sense of community and belonging.

Outcome

Sara decided to become more involved in her local community. She joined a neighbourhood parenting group and started participating in community events. Through these activities, Sara built a supportive network of friends and neighbours who understood her struggles. The community provided practical help, such as babysitting and carpooling, and emotional support through shared experiences and advice. This network enhanced Sara's sense of belonging and significantly reduced her stress. She felt more connected and supported, which positively impacted her mental health and overall well-being. The supportive community became a vital part of her life, illustrating the benefits of being part of a strong social network.

"These stories highlight the transformative power of a strong support system. Whether it's family, friends, mentors, or community, supportive relationships provide the foundation for resilience and well-being. By building and maintaining these connections, you can navigate life's challenges with greater confidence and strength."

Practical Exercises and Actionable Steps

Building Your Support Network

Identifying and Reaching Out to Potential Supporters

Building a support network starts with identifying the people who can offer you genuine support. Look for individuals who have shown care and interest in your well-being, such as family members, friends, colleagues, or mentors. Make a list of these potential supporters.

Once you've identified them, reach out and reconnect. This can be as simple as sending a friendly message or inviting them for a coffee. The goal is to rekindle the relationship and express your interest in mutual support. Be open about your desire to build a stronger support system and see if they are willing to be part of it.

Creating a Plan to Strengthen Existing Relationships

Strengthening existing relationships requires consistent effort and intentionality. Start by scheduling regular check-ins with your key supporters. This can be weekly calls, monthly meetups, or even just a consistent messaging routine. Show genuine interest in their lives and be there to support them as well.

Create a plan that includes:

Regular Communication: Schedule times to catch up and stay updated on each other's lives.

Shared Activities: Engage in activities that both of you enjoy, fostering a deeper connection.

Express Gratitude: Regularly show appreciation for their support, reinforcing the value of the relationship.

By actively reaching out and maintaining consistent communication, you can build a robust support network that provides mutual benefit.

Effective Communication Skills

Techniques for Active Listening and Empathetic Communication

Effective communication is the bedrock of strong relationships. Active listening involves fully concentrating, understanding, and responding thoughtfully to what the other person is saying. Here's how to practice it:

Give Full Attention: Put away distractions and focus entirely on the speaker.

Acknowledge and Reflect: Nod, use affirmations and reflect on what you've heard to show understanding.

Ask Open-Ended Questions: Encourage the speaker to share more by asking questions that cannot be answered with a simple yes or no.

Strategies for Expressing Needs and Offering Support

When it comes to expressing your needs, clarity and honesty are key. Use "I" statements to communicate your feelings and needs without sounding accusatory. For example, "I feel overwhelmed and could use some help with this project" is more effective than "You never help me with projects."

To offer support, be proactive and specific. Instead of saying, "Let me know if you need anything," offer concrete help like, "I can assist you with your project this weekend."

Practicing these communication techniques helps build trust and understanding, making your support network stronger and more effective.

Engaging in Community Activities

Finding and Participating in Community Groups and Activities

Engaging with your community can provide a rich source of support and connection. Start by identifying groups and activities that align with your interests and values. This could be local clubs, hobby groups, or social organizations. Websites like Meetup or local community centres often list various group activities.

Research Local Groups: Look for groups that match your interests, whether it's a book club, hiking group, or volunteer organization.

Attend Meetings Regularly: Consistent participation helps you build relationships and become a valued member of the group.

Be Open and Friendly: Approach new people with an open mind and show genuine interest in getting to know them.

Volunteering and Contributing to Your Community for Mutual Support

Volunteering is a powerful way to connect with others while making a positive impact. It fosters a sense of belonging and provides opportunities to meet like-minded individuals.

Choose a Cause You Care About: Find volunteer opportunities that resonate with you, whether it's helping at a food bank, mentoring youth, or participating in community cleanups.

Commit Regularly: Consistent involvement not only helps the cause but also builds deeper connections with fellow volunteers.

Share Your Skills: Offer your unique skills and talents to support the community. This can be anything from organizing events to providing professional expertise.

By actively engaging in community activities and volunteering, you expand your support network and create a sense of mutual support and camaraderie.

Chapter Summary

- Identifying Key Relationships: Recognizing family, friends, colleagues, and mentors as crucial parts of your support network.
- Building Supportive Relationships: Tips for cultivating trust, mutual respect, regular communication, and quality time.
- Balancing Give and Take: Ensuring reciprocity in relationships by providing and seeking support equally.
- Consistency and Reliability: Importance of being dependable and maintaining regular contact with your support network.
- Handling Conflicts: Effective communication and conflict resolution techniques, maintaining healthy boundaries.
- Nurturing Growth: Encouraging personal and mutual growth, celebrating successes, and supporting through challenges.

CHAPTER TEN

OVERCOMING SETBACKS AND MAINTAINING PROGRESS

Life is filled with setbacks. No matter how well you plan or how hard you work, obstacles and failures are inevitable. The real question is not whether you will encounter setbacks, but how you will respond to them. This chapter is dedicated to understanding how to overcome setbacks and maintain progress, even when the road gets tough.

Brief Overview of the Chapter's Focus

In this chapter, we will explore practical strategies for dealing with setbacks and the importance of persistence and consistency in achieving long-term success. We'll delve into techniques for reframing setbacks as opportunities, developing a problem-solving mindset, and building emotional resilience. Additionally, you'll hear inspirational stories of individuals who have faced significant challenges and emerged stronger and more successful. These stories will illustrate how persistence, support systems, and a positive mindset can turn obstacles into stepping stones.

Importance of Resilience and the Mindset Needed to Persist Through Challenges

Resilience is the ability to bounce back from adversity. It's a skill that can be developed and strengthened over time. Resilient people don't just survive setbacks; they thrive because of them. They view challenges as opportunities to learn and grow. This mindset is crucial for maintaining progress in the face of obstacles.

To persist through challenges, you need a mindset that embraces failure as part of the journey. This involves recognizing that setbacks are not permanent and that they do not define your potential. Instead, they are temporary detours that can lead to new insights and opportunities. Persistence requires a commitment to your goals and a willingness to keep moving forward, even when progress seems slow or difficult.

In the following sections, we will dive deep into strategies and tools to help you build resilience, stay persistent, and continue making progress despite setbacks. By adopting these approaches, you can turn challenges into catalysts for growth and success.

Strategies for Dealing with Setbacks

Understanding Setbacks

Setbacks are an inevitable part of any journey. They come in many forms: a failed project, a lost job, a missed opportunity, or a personal disappointment. These obstacles can be frustrating and disheartening, but they also offer valuable lessons.

Defining Setbacks and Their Common Sources

A setback is any event that disrupts your progress and pushes you off course. Common sources of setbacks include external factors like economic downturns, workplace politics, and unexpected personal issues. Internal factors such as self-doubt, fear of failure, and lack of preparation can also contribute to setbacks.

The Role of Setbacks in Personal Growth and Development

Setbacks play a crucial role in personal growth and development. They force you to re-evaluate your strategies, identify weaknesses, and develop new skills. When approached with the right mindset, setbacks can become powerful catalysts for growth. Embracing setbacks as part of the process allows you to learn, adapt, and ultimately become more resilient and capable.

Reframing Setbacks as Opportunities

The way you perceive setbacks significantly impacts your ability to overcome them. By changing your perspective, you can transform failures into opportunities for growth.

Techniques for Changing Your Perspective on Failures

Adopt a Growth Mindset: Embrace the belief that abilities and intelligence can be developed through dedication and hard work. View challenges as opportunities to grow rather than threats to your success.

Focus on What You Can Control: Instead of dwelling on what went wrong, concentrate on what you can do differently next time. This shift in focus empowers you to take proactive steps toward improvement.

Practice Gratitude: Acknowledge the lessons learned and the personal growth achieved through setbacks. Gratitude shifts your focus from loss to gain, making it easier to see the positive aspects of difficult experiences.

How to Identify Lessons and Opportunities Within Setbacks

Reflect on the Experience: Take time to analyze what happened and why. Identify specific factors that contributed to the setback and consider how you can address them in the future.

Ask Constructive Questions: Instead of asking, "Why did this happen to me?" ask, "What can I learn from this?" or "How can I use this experience to improve?"

Seek Feedback: Engage with mentors, colleagues, or friends to gain different perspectives on the setback. Their insights can help you identify areas for growth that you might have overlooked.

By reframing setbacks as opportunities, you can turn obstacles into valuable learning experiences that propel you forward.

Developing a Problem-Solving Mindset

A problem-solving mindset enables you to tackle setbacks with confidence and creativity. It involves approaching challenges systematically and focusing on finding solutions rather than getting bogged down by the problem itself.

Steps for Approaching Setbacks with a Problem-Solving Attitude

Stay Calm and Objective: When faced with a setback, take a step back and assess the situation calmly. Emotions can cloud judgment, so strive to maintain a clear and objective perspective.

Define the Problem: Clearly articulate the issue at hand. Understanding the root cause of the setback is essential for developing effective solutions.

Brainstorm Solutions: Generate a list of potential solutions without judging their feasibility initially. This encourages creative thinking and opens up a range of possibilities.

Evaluate and Select the Best Solution: Assess the pros and cons of each potential solution. Consider factors such as resources, time, and impact. Choose the solution that offers the most effective and practical resolution.

Implement and Monitor: Put the chosen solution into action and monitor its progress. Be prepared to make adjustments as needed based on feedback and results.

Examples of Problem-Solving Techniques in Action

SWOT Analysis: Use this tool to identify Strengths, Weaknesses, Opportunities, and Threats related to the setback. This comprehensive analysis helps in formulating strategic solutions.

Root Cause Analysis: Apply techniques like the "5 Whys" to dig deep into the underlying causes of the problem. Understanding the root cause ensures that solutions address the core issue rather than just the symptoms.

Developing a problem-solving mindset empowers you to navigate setbacks effectively, turning challenges into manageable tasks.

Building Emotional Resilience

Emotional resilience is the ability to adapt to and recover from stress, adversity, and setbacks. It involves managing your emotions effectively and maintaining a positive outlook even in difficult times.

Strategies for Managing Emotions During Setbacks

Practice Mindfulness: Mindfulness techniques such as meditation, deep breathing, and mindful journaling help you stay present and reduce stress. These practices improve emotional regulation and resilience.

Develop Emotional Awareness: Recognize and understand your emotions. Acknowledge how you feel without judgment, which helps you process emotions more constructively.

Seek Social Support: Connect with friends, family, or support groups to share your feelings and experiences. Social support provides comfort and perspective, making it easier to cope with setbacks.

The Importance of Self-Compassion and Mindfulness

Self-Compassion: Treat yourself with the same kindness and understanding you would offer a friend. Acknowledge that setbacks are a normal part of life and not a reflection of your worth or abilities.

Mindfulness: Stay present and focused on the current moment. Mindfulness helps you avoid getting overwhelmed by negative thoughts about the past or future, allowing you to handle setbacks more calmly and effectively.

Building emotional resilience equips you with the tools to manage stress and recover from setbacks, ensuring that you remain focused and motivated.

Creating a Support System for Setbacks

A strong support system is invaluable when facing setbacks. Surrounding yourself with supportive individuals provides emotional comfort, practical assistance, and valuable perspectives.

Utilizing Your Support Network to Navigate Challenges

Identify Key Supporters: Recognize the people in your life who offer genuine support. This can include family, friends, colleagues, and mentors.

Communicate Openly: Share your challenges and setbacks with your support network. Open communication fosters understanding and allows others to offer the help you need.

Ask for Help: Don't hesitate to reach out for assistance. Whether it's advice, a listening ear, or practical help, asking for support strengthens your network and helps you overcome setbacks more effectively.

Specific Ways Family, Friends, Mentors, and Communities Can Help

Family: Family members can provide a stable foundation of emotional support. They offer comfort, understanding, and a sense of belonging, which are crucial during tough times.

Friends: Friends offer a unique perspective and can help you see setbacks from different angles. They provide encouragement and motivation, helping you stay positive and focused.

Mentors: Mentors bring experience and wisdom to the table. They can offer strategic advice, share similar experiences, and guide you through challenges with practical solutions.

Communities: Being part of a community, whether it's a professional group, a hobby club, or an online forum, provides a broader support network. Communities offer diverse insights, resources, and collective encouragement.

"By leveraging your support system, you can navigate setbacks with greater resilience and resourcefulness. The combined strength of your network amplifies your ability to overcome challenges and continue making progress."

Importance of Persistence and Consistency

The Power of Persistence

How Persistence Leads to Long-Term Success

Persistence is the unwavering commitment to continue working toward your goals despite obstacles and setbacks. It's the ability to keep going, even when progress is slow or results are not immediately visible. Persistence fuels long-term success because it allows you to accumulate small, incremental gains that compound over time. Each effort builds upon the last, creating a snowball effect that leads to significant achievements.

When you persist, you develop resilience and adaptability. You learn to overcome challenges and find new solutions, which enhances your skills and knowledge. Persistence also builds mental toughness, enabling you to handle future obstacles with greater ease and confidence. Ultimately, the key to long-term success lies in your ability to stay the course and keep pushing forward, regardless of the difficulties you encounter.

Historical Examples of Persistence Leading to Breakthroughs

Thomas Edison: Edison is famous for his persistence in inventing the electric light bulb. He conducted over 1,000 experiments before finding the right filament. Edison's persistence exemplifies how repeated efforts and learning from failures can lead to groundbreaking success.

J.K. Rowling: Before achieving worldwide fame with the Harry Potter series, Rowling faced numerous rejections from publishers. Her persistence in submitting her manuscript eventually paid off, transforming her into one of the most successful authors in history.

Nelson Mandela: Mandela's persistent fight against apartheid in South Africa, despite being imprisoned for 27 years, led to significant social and political change. His unwavering commitment to justice and equality is a powerful example of persistence leading to monumental impact.

These historical figures show that persistence is often the key ingredient in turning vision into reality. By continuing to pursue their goals despite setbacks, they achieved remarkable success and left a lasting legacy.

Consistency as a Key to Success

The Role of Daily Habits and Routines in Maintaining Progress

Consistency is about maintaining regular and steady efforts toward your goals. It involves establishing daily habits and routines that keep you on track and moving forward. Consistency transforms small, repeated actions into significant progress over time.

Daily habits create a structure that makes it easier to stay focused and disciplined. For instance, consistently setting aside time each day for exercise, reading, or working on a project ensures that these activities become ingrained in your routine. This regularity reduces the mental effort required to initiate tasks and builds momentum that propels you toward your goals.

Practical Tips for Staying Consistent Even When Motivation Wanes

Set Clear and Specific Goals: Define what you want to achieve and break it down into manageable steps. Clear goals provide direction and make it easier to stay consistent.

Create a Routine: Establish a daily schedule that includes dedicated time for your key activities. Consistency in your routine helps you develop positive habits.

Track Your Progress: Use a journal or app to monitor your daily activities and progress. Seeing your progress can be motivating and reinforce the importance of staying consistent.

Simplify Your Tasks: Break tasks into smaller, more manageable parts. This makes it easier to get started and maintain momentum, even when motivation is low.

Reward Yourself: Celebrate small wins along the way. Rewards provide positive reinforcement and keep you motivated to continue your efforts.

Stay Accountable: Share your goals with a friend or join a group with similar objectives. Accountability increases your commitment to maintaining consistency.

Consistency builds a strong foundation for long-term success. By incorporating these tips, you can stay on track and make steady progress, even during times when motivation wanes.

Balancing Patience and Urgency

Finding the Right Balance Between Being Patient and Maintaining a Sense of Urgency

Achieving your goals requires a balance between patience and urgency. Patience involves understanding that progress takes time and being willing to persevere through slow periods. Urgency, on the other hand, motivates you to act promptly and make the most of your time.

Balancing these two elements ensures that you maintain steady progress without becoming complacent. It helps you stay motivated and focused while also recognizing that meaningful achievements often require sustained effort over time.

Strategies for Setting Realistic Timelines and Goals

Set SMART Goals: Ensure your goals are Specific, Measurable, Achievable, Relevant, and Time-bound. This framework helps you set realistic objectives and timelines.

Break Down Goals: Divide your larger goals into smaller, actionable steps. This makes them more manageable and allows you to track progress more effectively.

Prioritize Tasks: Focus on high-impact activities that move you closer to your goals. Use tools like the Eisenhower Matrix to prioritize tasks based on urgency and importance.

Adjust Your Timeline: Be flexible with your timelines. If you encounter setbacks or if progress is slower than expected, adjust your timeline rather than giving up on your goal.

Maintain a Sense of Urgency: Create deadlines for each step of your plan. Deadlines instil a sense of urgency and help you avoid procrastination.

Practice Patience: Recognize that setbacks and slow progress are part of the journey. Stay committed to your goals, even when results are not immediate.

> *"By balancing patience with urgency, you can maintain a steady pace toward your goals while staying motivated and focused. This balanced approach ensures that you make consistent progress without becoming overwhelmed or discouraged."*

Inspirational Stories

Story 1: Overcoming Career Setbacks

Background

John, a mid-level manager in a tech company, faced a significant career setback when his company underwent a major restructuring. His position was eliminated, leaving him jobless and uncertain about his future. The job market was tough, and John struggled with self-doubt and anxiety about his career prospects.

Strategies Used

John decided to approach his setback with persistence and a problem-solving mindset. He began by updating his skills and taking online courses to stay current with industry trends. John also reached out to his professional network for advice and support, leveraging connections to explore new opportunities. He remained proactive in his job search, applying to multiple positions and attending industry events to broaden his network.

Outcome

After several months of relentless effort, John secured a new position at a startup. The new role not only matched his skills but also offered greater growth potential. The experience taught John the value of persistence, continuous learning, and the importance of a strong support system. He emerged more resilient and confident, with a renewed sense of purpose in his career.

Story 2: Personal Health Challenges

Background

Sarah, a marketing executive, was diagnosed with a chronic illness that severely impacted her daily life. The diagnosis was a significant setback, causing physical pain and emotional distress. She struggled to manage her symptoms while maintaining her demanding job, leading to frustration and a feeling of helplessness.

Strategies Used

Sarah decided to reframe her health challenges as an opportunity to build resilience. She educated herself about her condition and developed a comprehensive management plan that included medication, lifestyle changes, and stress reduction techniques. Sarah also sought support from friends, family, and a local support group for people with similar health issues. She practiced mindfulness and meditation to help manage her emotional stress.

Outcome

With a proactive approach and strong support system, Sarah saw significant improvements in her health. She learned to manage her symptoms effectively, which allowed her to maintain her job and improve her quality of life. The experience gave her a new perspective on life, teaching her the importance of self-care, resilience, and the power of community support.

Story 3: Academic Failures to Success

Background

Tom, a college student, faced academic setbacks after failing several critical exams. The failures shook his confidence and led to anxiety about his future. He began to doubt his abilities and considered dropping out of college.

Strategies Used

Determined to turn his situation around, Tom adopted a strategy of consistency and persistence. He sought help from academic advisors and tutors to address his weaknesses. Tom implemented a structured study schedule, breaking down his coursework into manageable daily tasks. He also developed problem-solving skills to tackle difficult subjects and stayed consistent with his study routine, even when motivation was low.

Outcome

Over time, Tom's grades began to improve. He passed his exams and regained his confidence. The experience taught him the value of persistence and the importance of seeking help when needed. Tom's academic turnaround not only boosted his confidence but also prepared him for future challenges, both academically and professionally.

Story 4: Entrepreneurial Challenges

Background

Emily, an entrepreneur, faced significant setbacks when her first business venture failed. She lost a substantial amount of money and faced criticism from peers and investors. The failure was a major blow to her confidence and financial stability.

Strategies Used

Emily chose to view her entrepreneurial failure as a learning opportunity. She analyzed what went wrong, sought advice from successful entrepreneurs, and educated herself on better business practices. Emily leveraged her support network, including mentors and fellow entrepreneurs, for guidance and encouragement. She remained persistent, developing a new business plan that addressed the shortcomings of her previous venture.

Outcome

Emily's second venture was a success. Her persistence, combined with the lessons learned from her initial failure, led to a thriving business. She built a strong team, secured reliable investors, and created a sustainable business model. Emily's journey underscored the importance of persistence, leveraging support, and learning from setbacks. Her story serves as an inspiration to other entrepreneurs facing similar challenges.

"These stories highlight the transformative power of persistence, problem-solving, and support systems in overcoming setbacks. Each individual faced significant challenges but emerged stronger and more resilient. By adopting a positive mindset and leveraging available resources, they turned obstacles into opportunities for growth and success."

Practical Exercises and Actionable Steps

Reflecting on Past Setbacks

Exercise: Analyzing Past Setbacks to Identify Patterns and Lessons

Reflection is a powerful tool for personal growth. By analyzing past setbacks, you can identify patterns and lessons that will help you navigate future challenges more effectively.

Steps: Reflect, Write, and Discuss with a Trusted Person

Reflect: Set aside time to think about significant setbacks you've experienced. Consider what happened, how you responded, and the outcome.

Write: Document your reflections in a journal. Write about the circumstances, your reactions, and the lessons learned. Be honest and detailed.

Discuss: Share your reflections with a trusted friend, mentor, or family member. Discussing your experiences can provide new insights and reinforce the lessons learned.

By regularly reflecting on past setbacks, you can better understand your responses and develop strategies to handle future challenges more effectively.

Developing a Resilience Plan

Exercise: Creating a Plan to Handle Future Setbacks

A resilience plan prepares you to face future setbacks with confidence and clarity. It involves identifying potential challenges, developing strategies, and establishing a support system.

Steps: Identify Potential Challenges, Develop Strategies, and Establish a Support System

Identify Potential Challenges: Think about possible setbacks you might encounter in various areas of your life, such as career, health, or personal relationships. Write them down.

Develop Strategies: For each potential challenge, brainstorm strategies to address it. Consider problem-solving techniques, emotional resilience practices, and practical actions.

Establish a Support System: Identify people who can provide support during challenging times. This could include family, friends, mentors, or professional support groups. Make a list and keep it handy.

Having a resilience plan helps you feel more prepared and empowered to tackle setbacks as they arise, ensuring you stay on track toward your goals.

Implementing Daily Consistency Habits

Exercise: Building Habits that Promote Persistence and Consistency

Consistency is key to achieving long-term success. By developing daily habits that promote persistence, you can maintain progress even when motivation wanes.

Steps: Set Daily Goals, Track Progress, and Adjust as Needed

Set Daily Goals: Break down your larger goals into smaller, manageable daily tasks. Ensure these tasks are specific and achievable.

Track Progress: Use a journal, planner, or app to track your daily activities and progress. Regular tracking helps you stay accountable and identify patterns.

Adjust as Needed: Periodically review your progress and adjust your goals and habits as necessary. Flexibility allows you to adapt to changing circumstances and stay on course.

Example Routine:

Morning: Start with a quick review of your goals and set priorities for the day.

Midday: Check-in on your progress, take a short break, and adjust tasks if needed.

Evening: Reflect on what you accomplished, write down any lessons learned, and plan for the next day.

Consistency in your daily habits creates a strong foundation for persistence and progress. By setting clear goals, tracking your progress, and being adaptable, you build the resilience needed to overcome setbacks and continue moving forward.

Conclusion

Overcoming setbacks and maintaining progress requires a combination of persistence, resilience, and consistent effort. By understanding setbacks, reframing them as opportunities, developing a problem-solving mindset, building emotional resilience, and leveraging your support system, you can navigate challenges effectively. Implementing practical exercises like reflecting on past setbacks, developing a resilience plan, and maintaining daily consistency habits further strengthens your ability to stay on track.

The strategies and exercises discussed in this chapter are designed to be practical and actionable. Start by reflecting on your past experiences, create a resilience plan for future challenges, and establish daily habits that promote consistency. Remember, setbacks are a natural part of the journey. How you respond to them determines your success.

Chapter Summary

- Reframing Setbacks as Opportunities: Learn to view failures as chances to learn and grow, identifying valuable lessons and opportunities within them.
- Developing a Problem-Solving Mindset: Approach challenges with a systematic, solution-focused attitude to effectively overcome obstacles.
- Building Emotional Resilience: Manage emotions through strategies like mindfulness and self-compassion to bounce back from setbacks stronger.
- Creating a Support System for Setbacks: Utilize family, friends, mentors, and communities to navigate challenges and provide emotional and practical support.
- The Power of Persistence: Understand that persistence leads to long-term success by continually striving towards goals despite obstacles.
- Consistency as a Key to Success: Maintain daily habits and routines to ensure steady progress, even when motivation wanes.
- Balancing Patience and Urgency: Find the right balance between being patient and maintaining a sense of urgency to achieve goals efficiently.

Appendice

What Should You Read Next?

Thank you so much for taking the time to read Mental Pressure. It has been a pleasure sharing my work with you. If you are looking for something to read next, allow me to offer a suggestion. If you enjoyed Mental Pressure, then you may like my other writing as well. My latest articles are sent out in my free weekly newsletter. Subscribers are also the first to hear about my newest books and projects. Finally, in addition to my own work, each year I send out a reading list of my favourite books from other authors on a wide range of subjects. You can sign up at: rahuldwivedi.me/newsletter.

Worksheets and Self-Assessment Tools

Worksheet 1: Reflecting on Past Setbacks

1. **Identify a Significant Setback:** Describe a major setback you've faced.
2. **Analyze the Situation:** What were the circumstances leading to the setback?
3. **Emotional Response:** How did you feel at the time? What emotions did you experience?
4. **Actions Taken:** What steps did you take to address the setback?
5. **Lessons Learned:** What did you learn from this experience?
6. **Future Application:** How can these lessons be applied to future challenges?

Worksheet 2: Developing a Resilience Plan

1. **Potential Challenges:** List potential setbacks you might encounter in the

next year.

2. **Strategies:** For each potential challenge, write down at least two strategies to address it.
3. **Support System:** Identify individuals who can provide support for each type of setback.
4. **Action Steps:** Outline specific actions you will take when faced with these setbacks.
5. **Review and Adjust:** Schedule regular reviews of your resilience plan to adjust strategies as needed.

Worksheet 3: Implementing Daily Consistency Habits

Daily Goals: List three daily goals that align with your long-term objectives.

- **Habit Tracker:** Create a habit tracker to monitor your progress over a month.

  Day 1-7: Focus on establishing the habit.
  Day 8-14: Reinforce the habit and track consistency.
  Day 15-21: Identify any obstacles to maintaining the habit.
  Day 22-30: Adjust and solidify the habit.
  Reflection: At the end of each week, reflect on your progress and make necessary adjustments.

Self-Assessment Tool: Resilience and Consistency Evaluation

Rate Your Resilience: On a scale of 1 to 10, rate your ability to bounce back from setbacks.

Identify Strengths: What are your strengths in handling setbacks?
Identify Weaknesses: What areas need improvement?
Consistency Evaluation: How consistent are you in working toward your goals? Rate from 1 to 10.
Improvement Plan: Develop a plan to enhance your resilience and consistency based on the self-assessment.

Example of a Completed Worksheet: Reflecting on Past

Setbacks

1. **Identify a Significant Setback:** Failed to secure a promotion at work.
2. **Analyze the Situation:** Lack of required skills and poor interview performance.
3. **Emotional Response:** Felt disappointed, frustrated, and doubted my abilities.
4. **Actions Taken:** Took a course to develop necessary skills and sought feedback on interview performance.
5. **Lessons Learned:** Importance of continuous skill development and preparation for interviews.
6. **Future Application:** Regularly update skills and seek feedback to improve performance.

Example of a Completed Worksheet: Developing a Resilience Plan

- **Potential Challenges:** Facing a major project deadline while managing personal responsibilities.
- **Strategies:** Prioritize tasks, delegate responsibilities, and manage time effectively.
- **Support System:** Colleagues for professional support, family for personal support.
- **Action Steps:** Create a detailed project timeline, communicate needs to family and colleagues, and set up regular check-ins with support system.
- **Review and Adjust:** Monthly review of progress and adjustment of strategies as needed.

Call-to-action

Unlock Exclusive Bonus Chapters:

Thank you for reading "Mental Pressure." I hope you found the strategies and insights helpful in managing and reducing mental pressure in your life. To further support you on your journey, I have created exclusive bonus chapters available only on my website. These chapters are tailored to specific groups, providing targeted advice and strategies:

- ***Mental Pressure for Students***

- ***Mental Pressure for Working Professionals***

- ***Mental Pressure for Parents***

Visit www.**rahuldwivedi.me** to access these bonus chapters and additional resources designed to help you thrive in your unique situation.

Notes

In this section, you will find a comprehensive list of notes, references, and citations for each chapter in Mental Pressure. I believe this list will be helpful for most readers. However, scientific literature evolves over time, and references in this book may need updating. I also acknowledge that mistakes can happen—whether in attributing ideas or failing to give due credit. If you notice any errors or omissions, please email me at contact@rahuldwivedi.me so I can correct them promptly. For the most up-to-date endnotes and corrections, visit rahuldwivedi.me

Chapter 1

1. American Psychological Association - Understanding Acute Stress: APA - Stress
2. Journal of Occupational Health Psychology - Chronic Work-Related Stress: JOHP - Chronic Stress
3. National Institute of Mental Health - Traumatic Stress and PTSD: NIMH - PTSD
4. Richard Lazarus's cognitive appraisal theory: Psychology Today
5. McEwen, B. S. (2007). "Physiology and Neurobiology of Stress and Adaptation: Central Role of the Brain." Physiological Reviews
6. Sapolsky, R. M. (2004). "Why Zebras Don't Get Ulcers." Holt Paperbacks
7. National Institute of Mental Health: Anxiety Disorders: NIMH - Anxiety Disorders
8. Masten, A. S. (2014). "Ordinary Magic: Resilience in Development." Guilford Press
9. Health Psychology: Mindfulness Meditation and Cortisol: NIH - Health Psychology
10. General Hospital Psychiatry: MBSR and Mental Health: PubMed - MBSR
11. National Crime Records Bureau (NCRB): Student Suicides in India: NCRB

Chapter 2:

1. American Psychological Association: APA - Workplace Stress
2. National Institute for Occupational Safety and Health (NIOSH): NIOSH - Job Stress
3. National Center for Biotechnology Information (NCBI): NCBI - Academic Stress
4. The Lancet: The Lancet - Academic Pressure
5. Computers in Human Behavior: Study on FOMO and Social Media
6. World Health Organization (WHO): WHO - Economic Stress
7. Journal of Counseling Psychology: Perfectionism and Mental Health
8. Journal of Family Psychology: Family Dynamics and Stress
9. Journal of Psychosomatic Research: Chronic Illness and Health Anxiety
10. Centers for Disease Control and Prevention (CDC): Physical Activity and Health
11. Cognitive Therapy and Research: Cognitive Distortions and Anxiety

Chapter 3:

1. American Heart Association: Stress and Heart Disease
2. Psychological Bulletin: Chronic Stress and Immune Function
3. Gastroenterology: Stress and Gastrointestinal Health
4. National Institute of Mental Health (NIMH): Anxiety and Depression
5. The Journal of Neuroscience: Stress and Cognitive Decline
6. Journal of Clinical Sleep Medicine: Stress and Sleep Disorders
7. Substance Abuse and Mental Health Services Administration (SAMHSA): Stress and Substance Abuse
8. The American Journal of Clinical Nutrition: Stress and Eating Disorders
9. Psychological Science: Stress and Risky Behaviors

Chapter 4:

1. American Psychological Association - Definition of Triggers and How They Impact Mental Pressure: APA - Stress: The Different Kinds of Stress
2. National Institutes of Health - The Role of Awareness in Managing Stress: NIH - Mindfulness in Practice

3. Healthline - High Job Demands and Deadlines: Healthline - The Effects of Stress on Your Body

4. Harvard Business Review - Lack of Control and Autonomy: HBR - What Great Managers Do to Engage Employees

5. Mayo Clinic - Interpersonal Conflicts and Workplace Bullying: Mayo Clinic - Workplace Bullying: How to Spot It and Stop It

6. National Center for Biotechnology Information - Academic Workload and Exam Pressure: NCBI - Stress and Academic Performance

7. American Psychological Association - Competition and High Expectations: APA - Stress in America: Generation Z

8. Education Week - Lack of Support and Guidance: Education Week - The Importance of Academic Advising

9. National Institutes of Health - Social Relationships and Peer Pressure: NIH - Peer Pressure: Its Influence on Teens and Decision Making

10. American Psychological Association - Financial Instability and Responsibilities: APA - Stress in America: Coping with Change

Chapter 5:

1. Mayo Clinic - Benefits of Physical Activity: Mayo Clinic - Exercise: 7 benefits of regular physical activity

2. American Heart Association - Types of Exercise: AHA - The Importance of Physical Activity

3. Harvard Health - Actionable Steps: Harvard Health - The secret to better health — exercise

4. Forbes - Benefits of Effective Time Management: Forbes - Time Management Tips That Work

5. Mind Tools - Techniques for Better Time Management: Mind Tools - Time Management

6. Verywell Mind - Actionable Steps: Verywell Mind - Time Management Tips

7. American Psychological Association - Importance of Social Support: [APA - The importance of social support](https://www.apa.org/news/press/releases/stress/

Chapter 6:

1. J.K. Rowling – From Struggling Single Mother to Bestselling Author: Biography of J.K. Rowling
2. Malala Yousafzai – Champion for Girls' Education: Malala Fund
3. Nick Vujicic – Life Without Limbs: Life Without Limbs
4. Bethany Hamilton – Overcoming the Odds in Surfing: Bethany Hamilton's Official Website

Chapter 7:

1. Harvard Study on Mindfulness and Stress Reduction: Harvard Medical School
2. University of Massachusetts Study on MBSR: UMass Memorial Health
3. University of California, Santa Barbara Study: UC Santa Barbara
4. Medical College of Georgia Research: Augusta University
5. University of Wisconsin-Madison Study: Center for Healthy Minds
6. Emory University Studies: Emory Health Sciences
7. Mindful Breathing Guide: Mindful.org
8. Integrating Mindful Breathing into Daily Routine: Harvard Health
9. Benefits of Loving-Kindness Meditation: Psychology Today
10. Techniques for Mindful Walking: Greater Good Science Center
11. Benefits of Mindful Walking: Harvard Health
12. Mindfulness Techniques for Anxiety: Anxiety and Depression Association of America
13. Mindfulness and Productivity Case Study: Harvard Business Review
14. Meditation and Emotional Healing: American Psychological Association

Chapter 8:

1. Explanation and Practical Use: MindTools - The Eisenhower Matrix
2. Overview and Implementation: Brian Tracy - The ABCDE Method
3. Introduction and Tips: Calendar - Time Blocking 101

4. Example and Benefits: Todoist - How to Use Time Blocking
5. Explanation and Benefits: Francesco Cirillo - The Pomodoro Technique
6. How to Use: Lifehack - How to Use the Pomodoro Technique

Chapter 9:

1. Brené Brown - The Gifts of Imperfection: Brené Brown
2. Sheryl Sandberg and Adam Grant - Option B: Option B
3. Matthew D. Lieberman - Social: Why Our Brains Are Wired to Connect: Amazon
4. Brené Brown - Daring Greatly: Brené Brown
5. Sebastian Junger - Tribe: On Homecoming and Belonging: Sebastian Junger
6. Vivek H. Murthy - Together: The Healing Power of Human Connection in a Sometimes Lonely World: Vivek H. Murthy
7. Dale Carnegie - How to Win Friends and Influence People: Dale Carnegie

Chapter 10:

1. Angela Duckworth - Grit: The Power of Passion and Perseverance
2. Carol S. Dweck - Mindset: The New Psychology of Success
3. Charles Duhigg - The Power of Habit
4. Ryan Holiday - The Obstacle Is the Way: The Timeless Art of Turning Trials into Triumph
5. Sheryl Sandberg - Lean In: Women, Work, and the Will to Lead
6. Viktor E. Frankl - Man's Search for Meaning
7. James Clear - Atomic Habits
8. Carol Dweck - Mindset: The New Psychology of Success
9. Angela Duckworth - Grit: The Power of Passion and Perseverance
10. Ryan Holiday - The Obstacle Is the Way: The Timeless Art of Turning Trials into Triumph